GALILEO GALILEI
1564–1642 •
Discovered law of pendulum motion

CAROLUS LINNAEUS
• 1707–1778
Classified the plant
and animal kingdoms

SIGMUND FREUD
• 1856–1939
Started psychoanalysis

GREGOR JOHANN MENDEL
1822–1884 •
Discovered principles of heredity

BARON ERNEST RUTHERFORD
1871–1937 •
Contributed to knowledge of
radioactivity and atomic structure

GUGLIELMO MARCONI
• 1874–1937
invented the wireless telegraph

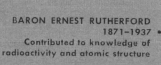

LOUIS AGASSIZ
• 1807–1873
Investigated glacial motion
and marine life

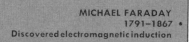

MICHAEL FARADAY
1791–1867 •
Discovered electromagnetic induction

SIR ISAAC NEWTON
• 1642–1727
Discovered laws of light,
gravity, motion and color

ALBERT EINSTEIN
1879–1955 •
Conceived the Theory of Relativity

WILHELM KONRAD ROENTGEN
• 1845–1923
Discovered X-rays

ALEXANDER GRAHAM BELL
1847–1922 •
Invented
the telephone

JOSEPH LISTER
• 1827–1912
Started antiseptic surgery

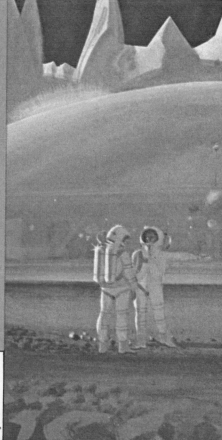

# YOUNG PEOPLE'S
# SCIENCE
## ENCYCLOPEDIA

*Edited by the Staff of*
NATIONAL COLLEGE OF EDUCATION, Evanston, Ill.

### ASSOCIATE EDITORS

HELEN J. CHALLAND, B.E., M.A., PH.D.
Chairman, Science Department, National
College of Education

DONALD A. BOYER, B.S., M.S., PH.D.
Science Education Consultant, Winnetka
Public Schools, Winnetka, Ill., Science,
National College of Education

W. RAY RUCKER, B.A., M.A., ED.D.
Former Dean of the College, National College of Education

### EDITORIAL CONSULTANTS
#### ON THE STAFF OF NATIONAL COLLEGE OF EDUCATION

Elizabeth R. Brandt, B.A., M.Ed.

Eugene B. Cantelupe, B.A., M.F.A., Ph.D.

John H. Daugherty, B.S., M.A.

Irwin K. Feinstein, B.S., M.A., Ph.D.

Mary Gallagher, A.B., M.A., Ph.D.

Beatrice B. Garber, A.B., M.S., Ph.D.

Robert R. Kidder, A.B., M.A., Ph.D.

Jean C. Kraft, B.S., M.A., Ph.D.

Elise P. Lerman, B.A., B.F.A., M.F.A.

Mary-Louise Neumann, A.B., B.S. in L.S.

Lavon Rasco, B.A., M.A., Ph.D.

### SPECIAL SUBJECT AREA CONSULTANTS

Krafft A. Ehricke, B.A.E., H.L.D.

Charles B. Johnson, B.S., M.A., M.S.

Raymond J. Johnson, B.B.A., Senior
Certificate in Industrial Engineering

Norma R. Rucker, B.S.

H. Kenneth Scatliff, M.D.

Ray C. Soliday, B.A., B.S., M.A.
(Deceased)

Fred R. Wilkin, Jr., B.S., M.Ed.

### THE STAFF

| | | |
|---|---|---|
| PROJECT DIRECTOR | · | WALLACE B. BLACK |
| COORDINATING EDITOR | · | JEAN F. BLASHFIELD |
| ART DIRECTOR | · | BEN ROSEN |
| PHOTO AND ART EDITOR | · | MARTHA O'ROURKE |
| PRODUCTION EDITOR | · | ORLANDO T. CURCIO |

# YOUNG PEOPLE'S
# SCIENCE
# ENCYCLOPEDIA

*Edited by the Staff of*

## NATIONAL COLLEGE OF EDUCATION
Evanston, Illinois

## VOLUME 7
## EM-FL

 CHILDRENS PRESS, CHICAGO

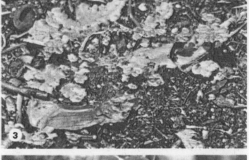

## SOME EMBRYOPHYTES

1—HORSETAIL
2—BLACK-EYED SUSAN
3—LIVERWORT
4—DEERHORN CACTUS
5—SILVER MAPLE
6—CLUB MOSS
7—FERN
8—FIR TREE
9—MOSS

**Embryophyta** (em-bree-AH-fuh-tuh) *Embryo* means the beginning of a living thing. *Phyta* is the Greek word meaning "plants." All of the plants in the world are grouped into two large subkingdoms. The THALLOPHYTA, algae and fungi, are a group that do not have embryos. The embryophytes do.

The embryophytes have several other characteristics that are different from those of most of the lower subkingdom. They have many-celled (multicellular) sex organs which produce the sex cells (gametes). With the exception of the group of *bryophytes,* they possess specialized conducting cells (XYLEM and PHLOEM) which transport raw materials and food throughout the plant. They have openings (stomata) on the leaves for the purpose of exchanging gases with the atmosphere. These changes which have occurred in the higher plants have enabled them to adapt to a land environment.

Plants that have in their life cycles an embryo of some kind are classed as embryo-

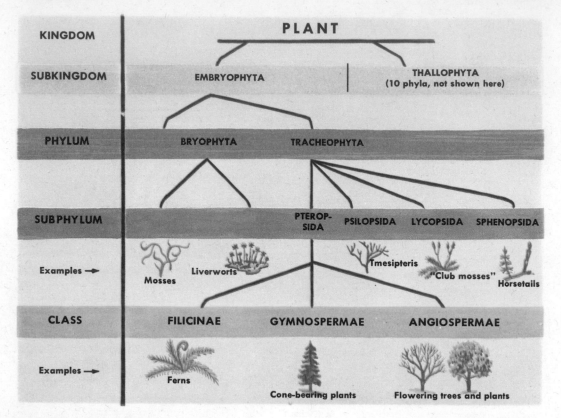

phytes. As they develop into plants with different characteristics, they are further divided into two groups, BRYOPHYTA and TRACHEOPHYTA.

Bryophytes are the mosses and the liverworts, small plants that grow in moist, shaded places. They manufacture their own food and can continue to grow if there is moisture in the air. To reproduce themselves, they need rain or other water. They have no special cells to carry dissolved substances from one part to another, though they have stem-like and leaf-like parts. Bryophytes have no true roots, stems, or leaves.

Tracheophytes possess roots, stems, and leaves, and most of them grow in the soil. They have vascular tissue which carries dissolved substances up and down, and the plants are usually upright in growth.

There are four subphyla in the phylum *Tracheophyta. Psilopsids* are plants having the simplest conducting systems. They have no common name, but they are interesting as "living fossils," for botanists believe that their nearest known relatives have been extinct for at least 300 million years. Psilotum is found in Florida, Bermuda, and Hawaii. Tmesipteris grows in Australia and the Philippines.

The second subphylum of the tracheophytes is *Lycopsida,* the CLUB MOSSES. The third subphylum is *Sphenopsida,* the HORSETAILS.

The fourth subphylum is *Pteropsida.* This grouping has three classes: Class *Filicineae* (the ferns), Class *Gymnospermae* (the conifers, trees that produce cones), and Class *Angiospermae* (the flowering plants). All of the pteropsids are called the "leafy plants." The last two classes, the gymnosperms and the angiosperms, are called the "higher tracheophytes." All of the other classes are called "lower tracheophytes." From the simple forms of the lower tracheophytes, botanists gain, in their search for more data on the life histories of all plants.

Gymnosperms and angiosperms, the "seed plants," provide man with food and shade and are necessary to his well-being.

Gymnosperms have cones to hold their seeds, as have evergreen trees. The seeds fall out through the scales of the cones. The word *gymnos* means "naked" and *sperm* means "seed" in Greek. In angiosperms the seed is enclosed in a fruit which develops after the flower.                P. G. B.

SEE ALSO: ANGIOSPERMS; GYMNOSPERMS; PLANT TISSUES; PLANTS, CLASSIFICATION OF

**Emerald** The emerald is a precious stone of a grassy green color. It is transparent, not brilliant or fiery. Its value depends on its color, size, and freedom from flaws.

Emerald is a form of BERYL, a silicate of aluminum and beryllium. The presence of CHROMIUM in the silicate causes the green color. Emerald is a soft stone, usually cut in a square or rectangular shape.

Emeralds are found in the Ural Mountains of Russia; in Colombia, South America; and in North Carolina. Fine emerald GEMS are more costly than fine diamonds.     C. L. K.

J. Daniel Willems

**A cut emerald gem**

**Emery** see Corundum

**Emu** see Birds, flightless

**Emulsion** When oil and water are mixed together in such a way that the little droplets of oil cannot be seen in the liquid, the product is an emulsion. An emulsion may also be the opposite—droplets of water that are so well mixed into oil that they cannot be seen.

Homogenized MILK is a good example of an emulsion. The particles of cream are mixed into the milk to form the emulsion. Mayonnaise is emulsified, while vinegar-and-oil salad dressings are not. Some medicines, such as CASTOR OIL, are emulsified so they are more pleasant to taste.     J. D. B.
SEE ALSO: SOLUTION

**Enamel** see Paint, Teeth

**Encyst** see Parasites

✳ **THINGS TO DO**

**WHAT IS AN EMULSION?**

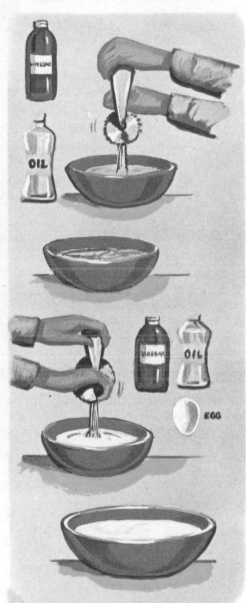

1  Beat one teaspoon of vinegar and four teaspoons of salad oil together. Let them stand for a few minutes.

2  This is not an emulsion because the oil and vinegar separate.

3  Now beat an egg and a teaspoon of vinegar together. Add four teaspoons of oil and beat again.

4  This mixture is an emulsion. All the ingredients stay mixed together.
                    J.D.B.

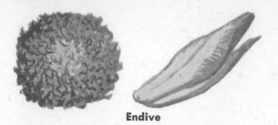

Endive

**Endive** Endive is an Old World plant which has been grown for less than 2000 years. This herb is a salad green still more popular in Europe than in the United States.

There are two kinds of plants which are called endive. The *escarole* is an annual or biennial with white or purple flowers. It is native to India. It looks like lettuce with curly-edged leaves. The outer leaves are green while the inner are white. The heads are tied up so they are *blanched* (bleached by keeping out the sun).

The other plant is *Witloof* CHICORY or French endive. It is a perennial used as greens in Europe.                         H. J. C.

**Endocrine glands** (ENN-doh-krinn) In man and other complex animals, there is a group of special body parts called *endocrine glands*. They make very important chemical substances for the body. Endocrine, loosely defined, means "inside leakage." These glands that make the liquid chemicals do let them "leak" right into the BLOOD. They have no tubes or ducts which collect and carry these chemicals. Glands that do have such ducts are called *exocrine* glands. As the blood flows through the small blood vessels in the endocrine glands, the chemicals pass from the cells of the gland into the blood vessels. Then, these chemicals are carried around in the blood to all parts of the body. These chemicals are important because they tell many parts of the body what to do and how fast or how slow to work.

The endocrine system is made of many different glands that specialize in making and giving off liquids needed by the body. Each gland makes its own kind of chemicals, and each chemical has a different job to do. These important chemicals have a special name. They are called *hormones*. Most of the important hormones are made by four kinds of glands: the ADRENAL GLANDS, the thyroid gland, the PARATHYROID glands, and the pituitary gland.

The PITUITARY gland controls the other endocrine glands. For this reason, the pituitary is called "the master gland." By means of the chemical messengers—the hormones—the endocrine glands control many important activities of the body. The THYROID regulates the rate at which the body uses energy. The pituitary, in addition to controlling the other endocrine glands, also influences the overall growth rate to make persons dwarfs, normal, or giants. These are just a few of the functions of the all-important endocrine system.

Many important hormones are produced by the exocrine glands. The GONADS, for example, help boys and girls develop the features of men and women. The PANCREAS controls the blood sugar.            R. S. C.

SEE ALSO: METABOLISM

**Endoderm** Endoderm is the inner of the three primary germ layers formed during the early embryonic development of a multicellular animal. From it come the lining of most of the alimentary canal and the chief digestive organs.

SEE: CLEAVAGE, EMBRYOLOGY

**Endoskeleton** Endoskeleton is the internal SKELETON or supporting structure of bones and cartilage characteristic of the vertebrates. It includes the vertebral column, ribs, skull, and the pectoral and pelvic girdles.

**Endothermic** Endothermic is a term describing a chemical reaction in which HEAT is continuously absorbed and must be supplied to keep the reaction going. An example is the reaction of nitrogen and oxygen to form nitric oxide.

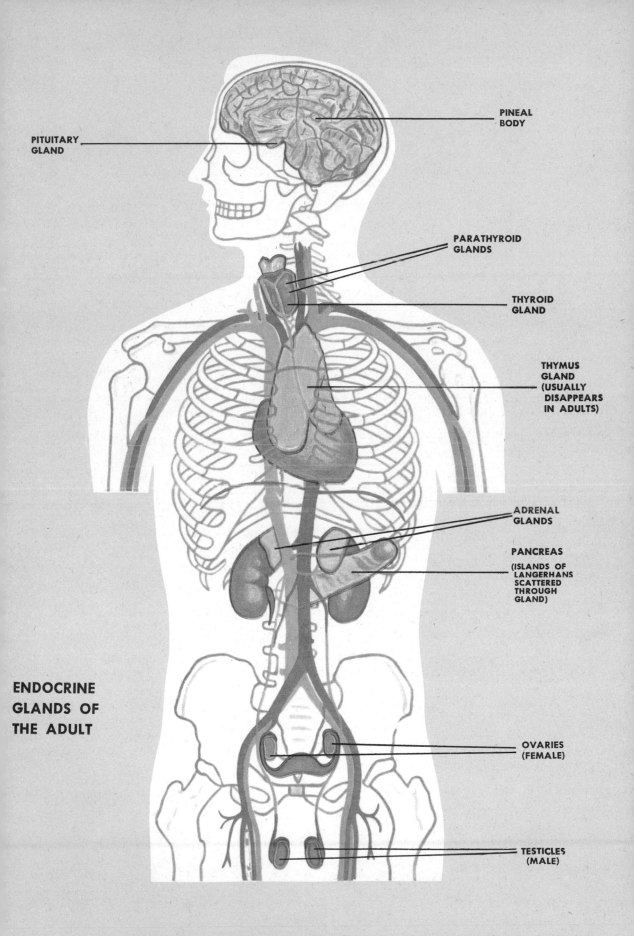

PINEAL
BODY

PITUITARY
GLAND

PARATHYROID
GLANDS

THYROID
GLAND

THYMUS
GLAND
(USUALLY
DISAPPEARS
IN ADULTS)

ADRENAL
GLANDS

PANCREAS
(ISLANDS OF
LANGERHANS
SCATTERED
THROUGH
GLAND)

ENDOCRINE
GLANDS OF
THE ADULT

OVARIES
(FEMALE)

TESTICLES
(MALE)

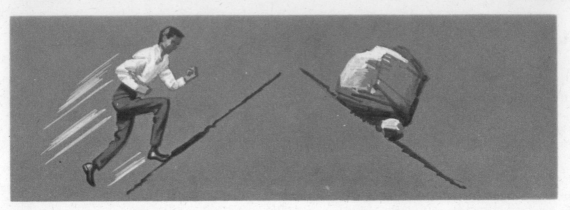

A boy running up the hill shows kinetic energy. The balanced rock, ready to roll, has potential energy

**Energy** Energy is the ability to do work. Energy is needed for a person to work, to jump, to run, to eat and so forth. Energy is needed for plants and animals to grow. It is present in another form in the electricity which lights lamps and makes television sets produce pictures. Energy is in the coal or oil that is burned for fuel in furnaces and in the engines of cars and airplanes.

### KINDS OF ENERGY

There are many different kinds of energy in the world around man. Some of them are chemical, mechanical, heat, gravitational, electrical, biological, radiant, and atomic. In addition to these *types* of energy, there are also two different energy *states*. One such state is called *kinetic energy* and the other *potential energy*. Kinetic energy can be called the "moving energy." This energy can be shown when a boy is running or when water is pouring down a waterfall. Potential energy is "stored" energy. It is that energy stored in a watch spring which is all coiled up, or in a large stone just ready to drop from the top of a hill. Kinetic energy can then be described as the energy possessed by a system due to its *motion*. Potential energy is the energy possessed by a system or an object due to its *position*.

There are a variety of potential energies, just as there are varieties of kinetic energies. As examples: there is mechanical potential energy in the wound spring of a clock or a stretched bowstring. There is gravitational potential energy in anything lifted against the pull of gravity, such as a stone lifted by a person. There is chemical potential energy in almost every known substance, since there is hardly anything known which will not react with some chemical agent and release its energy. There is electrical potential energy stored in electrical CONDENSERS.

### CONSERVATION OF ENERGY

Although one form of energy may be converted easily into another, such as potential to kinetic or chemical to electrical, the total amount of energy *always remains the same*. In other words, energy is neither created nor destroyed in any given system. This last statement is called the *law of conservation of energy*. Another way to state this law would be to say that for every amount of energy of a given type that disappears, the same amount of energy of another type appears, or the same total amount of a variety of types of energy appear. A further explanation can be seen from the following. A bullet leaves a gun with a certain kinetic energy. As it flies through the air, some of its energy is lost, or converted to heat energy due to its friction with the air. As the bullet

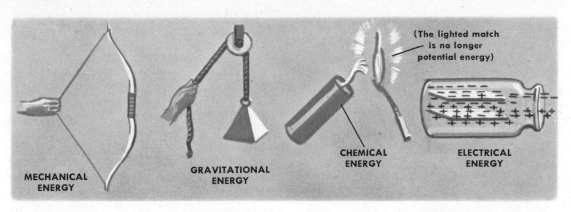

(The lighted match is no longer potential energy)

MECHANICAL ENERGY     GRAVITATIONAL ENERGY     CHEMICAL ENERGY     ELECTRICAL ENERGY

**Each of the forms of potential energy can instantly be converted to kinetic energy**

strikes its target, more energy is converted to sound and light. Heat will also be developed in the target, while fragments of the bullet will carry away some energy. If all of these "pieces" of lost or converted energy are totalled, they will equal the original kinetic energy with which the bullet was fired.

According to EINSTEIN'S theories, which are too complicated to detail here, there is also a relationship between matter and energy which deals with conservation of both. It is now known, by observing radioactive decomposition, that matter may also be converted to energy. An equation was created to show that this conversion takes place without loss:

$$E = mc^2,$$

where $E$, the energy, is equal to $m$, the mass or weight loss during the radioactive decomposition multiplied by $c^2$, the speed of light squared.

### THE HUMAN BODY AND ENERGY

The human body may be likened to a machine in its use of energy to perform its daily work. The energy for this work comes from CARBOHYDRATES, FATS, and PROTEINS, which are broken down in the body and their potential energy transferred. Some of the energy "captured" is used to do work inside the body and some of it is used to do work outside the body. This means that energy is needed for inside work, such as pumping blood, while a good portion of that energy is needed for doing outside work, such as walking, carrying packages and climbing stairs. The conservation law also seems to hold true for the body. If a person were to spend a day in a controlled room, it could be proved that the energy in the food eaten would be converted to an equal amount of heat energy, due to the internal and external work done by the person.

### CONSERVATION OF ENERGY

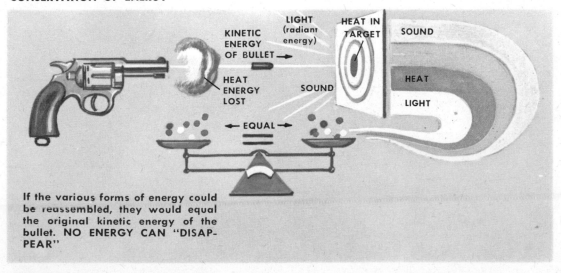

KINETIC ENERGY OF BULLET →    LIGHT (radiant energy)    HEAT IN TARGET    SOUND

HEAT ENERGY LOST    SOUND    HEAT    LIGHT

← EQUAL →

If the various forms of energy could be reassembled, they would equal the original kinetic energy of the bullet. NO ENERGY CAN "DISAPPEAR"

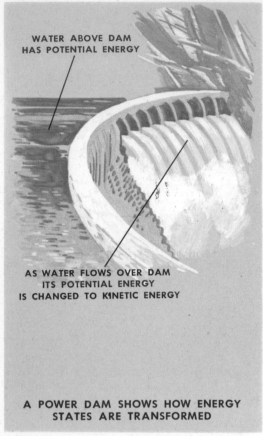

A POWER DAM SHOWS HOW ENERGY
STATES ARE TRANSFORMED

**Water going over a dam has usable energy**

## POTENTIAL AND KINETIC ENERGY

In order to be of some use, potential energy must be changed into kinetic energy. Water flowing over the edge of a dam, for example, has its potential energy "built-in" by the fact that work was necessary to lift it to the top of this dam. As the water flows over the top, its potential energy is being changed to kinetic energy. By the time it reaches the river below, all the potential energy is changed to kinetic. At any time in between the top and the bottom, however, the sum of the two energies is always equal to the total potential energy at the start, which is in turn equal to the kinetic energy at the end. This is another proof of the law of conservation of energy.

Conversion of kinetic energy into potential can be illustrated by the WINDMILL. The kinetic energy of the wheel as it spins can lift water and store it in a tank. The work done in lifting the water is stored as potential energy in the water. If the water is allowed to fall back to earth, this potential energy is again converted to kinetic energy.

Potential energy of an elevated body may be calculated from the formula:

$$P.E. = mgh,$$

where $P.E.$, the potential energy, is equal to $m$, the mass, multiplied by $g$, the acceleration due to gravity, multiplied by $h$, the vertical distance through which the mass is lifted. For kinetic energy, the following formula can be used:

$$K.E. = \tfrac{1}{2}mv^2,$$

where $K.E.$, the kinetic energy, is equal to $\tfrac{1}{2}m$, the mass, multiplied by $v^2$, the square of the speed at which the mass is moving. The units of measurement used in the above formulas are as follows:

| | English System | Metric System |
|---|---|---|
| $K.E.,$ | | |
| $P.E.$ | foot-poundals | joules |
| $m$ | pounds | kilograms |
| $g$ | feet per second per second | meters per second per second |
| $h$ | feet | meters |
| $v$ | feet per second | meters per second |

## CHEMICAL AND ELECTRICAL ENERGY

In the transforming of chemical energy into electrical energy, certain chemical reactions involve parts of the atoms of the elements in chemicals known as ELECTRONS. When these electrons are transferred from one chemical to another, an electric current can be set up. As an example, if two metal bars, such as zinc and copper, are partially immersed in a sulfuric acid solution, a

**The wheel's kinetic energy lifts water to the tank. The water then has potential energy**

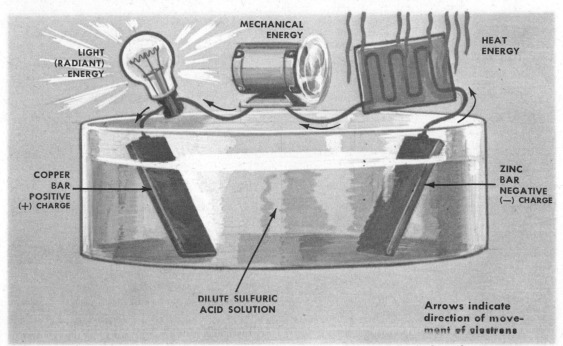

**LIGHT (RADIANT) ENERGY**

**MECHANICAL ENERGY**

**HEAT ENERGY**

**COPPER BAR POSITIVE (+) CHARGE**

**ZINC BAR NEGATIVE (—) CHARGE**

**DILUTE SULFURIC ACID SOLUTION**

**Arrows indicate direction of movement of electrons**

Electrons transfer from one chemical to another to produce light, mechanical, or heat energy. The energy conversion making this possible was discovered by Count Alessandro Volta

chemical reaction takes place. If the parts of these bars that are above the surface of the acid solution are connected to each other by a wire, it will be found that an electric current will flow through this wire. This conversion of chemical energy to electrical energy was discovered by VOLTA. This conversion system is today called the *voltaic cell,* in his honor. Modifications of this simple system are used as batteries in automobiles, flashlights, and many other places where ELECTRICITY is necessary and cannot be obtained from a main line.

The electrical energy transformed from chemical energy, as described above, can be used to do a great number of things. If the source of electrical energy is connected properly, it can light a lamp and therefore transfer part of its energy to light energy. The electrical source can be connected to a motor and transfer energy to mechanical energy. When an electrical source is connected to a toaster, all or most of the energy is converted to heat energy. Electricity is purchased from the local electric company as electric energy. As shown above, the JOULE is the unit of energy. The term WATT is a unit of power. This unit is used to rate light bulbs according to the amount of power they use. The watt means that one

joule of energy per second is being used up. The KILOWATT-HOUR is also a unit of energy derived from the equation:

*energy = power × time.* The kilowatt-hour is the unit used in calculating an electric bill.

Another form of electric energy is the familiar radio wave. This energy is transmitted from antennas into space and picked up by RADIO receivers.

### HEAT ENERGY

Heat energy is also obtained through the conversion of other sources of energy. The SUN is the earth's main source of heat energy, and its energy stems from nuclear fusion reactions occurring on its surface. These, of course, involve chemical energy converting to heat energy. Another source of heat energy comes from geysers and volcanoes below the earth's surface. The energy derived from chemicals in the form of heat is well known in the fuels used to heat homes and run automobiles. In addition there is the "fuel" called food which is broken down chemically in the body to produce heat energy. Mechanical energy also can produce heat when it runs into difficulties in the form of FRICTION. Electrical energy produces heat for a whole range of appliances such as toasters, irons, heating pads and others.

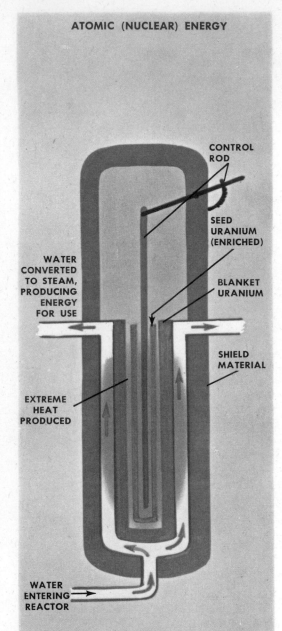

ATOMIC (NUCLEAR) ENERGY

CONTROL ROD

SEED URANIUM (ENRICHED)

WATER CONVERTED TO STEAM, PRODUCING ENERGY FOR USE

BLANKET URANIUM

SHIELD MATERIAL

EXTREME HEAT PRODUCED

WATER ENTERING REACTOR

Great amounts of energy are produced by the fission (splitting of the nucleus) of atoms. Above is a diagram of a thermal nuclear reactor of the pressurized water type. Hot water under pressure enters the reactor; the fission of uranium atoms then produces so much heat that water is changed to steam. This is done in the coils of a heat exchanger (not shown). The steam drives turbines or other machinery. The control rod is made of cadmium, or some similar element. It absorbs the neutrons of atomic nuclei without itself being changed. Therefore, it is used to slow down, or speed up, the reaction

## NUCLEAR ENERGY

Probably the greatest source of energy to produce heat is NUCLEAR ENERGY. Just within the past few years nuclear energy has been put to work for peaceful purposes. Nuclear energy is now being used to produce electrical energy at the Dresden plant south of Chicago. This electrical energy can, in turn, do the great number of jobs that electricity can do. Nuclear energy has also been put to work as fuel for the atomic SUBMARINES. Since a small amount of fuel, usually uranium (element 92), does a much more efficient job in producing energy than coal or oil, such submarines are able to go great distances for long periods of time without refueling. According to the Atomic Energy Commission in 1955, the amount of uranium and other radioactive elements obtained up to that time was enough to supply the world's energy needs for the next 2000 years.

## TRANSFER OF ENERGY

There are several ways in which energy can be moved along a given course. Electrical energy is moved through a wire by means of electrons. Heat energy is transferred from a bowl of hot soup through a spoon out to the end of its handle by the motion of invisible molecules of the metal in the spoon. The wind can transfer its energy to a lake, filling it full of rough waves. The energy involved in sound is carried along by another kind of wave and actually sets up vibrations in the ear, which are heard as sound. The sun's energy and electrical energy, in the form of radio waves, are also carried along by waves. These forms of energy which travel by waves cannot be seen, heard, or felt until they reach their destination and change forms.

Just as the various forms of energy can be converted to heat energy, heat itself can be converted to other forms of energy. When gasoline is burned in an automobile ENGINE, for example, the heat energy is changed to mechanical energy to work the pistons and crankshaft. A device called a *thermocouple* is acted upon by heat energy to start electric currents flowing. The heat energy of every single thing in the universe is constantly being converted to radiant energy and eventually being lost to outer space. Heat energy is not a measurement of temperature alone, but also depends upon the amount of material present. As an example, a full cup of

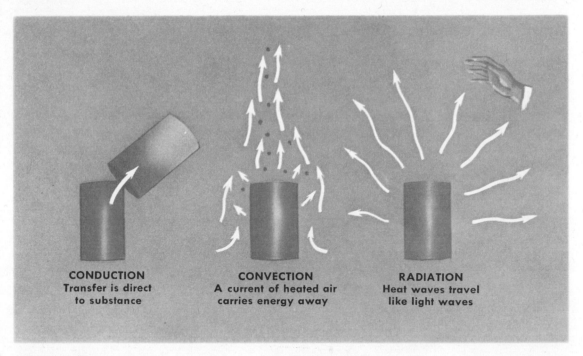

| CONDUCTION | CONVECTION | RADIATION |
|---|---|---|
| Transfer is direct to substance | A current of heated air carries energy away | Heat waves travel like light waves |

These principles of transfer of energy are used daily in most homes. Food is cooked by conduction, refrigeration is obtained by convection and homes are heated by radiation

water at a temperature of 100° F will have twice the heat energy of half a cup at the same temperature. Heat energy can be transferred easily from one object to another in any one of three different ways. These three ways of transferring heat are called conduction, convection and radiation. *Conduction* of heat energy works through direct contact of the heat source and the body accepting the heat. CONVECTION of heat energy takes place by the actual movement of a heated liquid or gas, such as air. The heated liquid or gas then makes contact with the object accepting the heat. The third transfer process is called RADIATION, which does not use direct contact in order to transfer heat energy. Radiant energy, such as that from the sun, travels through empty space at 186,000 miles per second. When the rays strike an object, this energy is again converted to heat energy. The radiant energy from the sun is an essential part of the process of PHOTOSYNTHESIS, which produces chlorophyll in plants giving them their green color.

### ENERGY AND WORK

Count Rumford (Benjamin Thompson) is considered to be the discoverer of the relationship between heat energy and work. Thompson found that large amounts of heat

were developed in the boring of holes to make cannons. This type of work was done with horses and it involved a great deal of friction. Thompson found that the faster the horses were made to work, that is the more energy they used, the more heat was developed in the particles of metal that were being bored out. He was able to demonstrate this by putting these particles in water and observing the temperature rise in the water with a thermometer. It was shown that the more energy the horses used, the higher the temperature of the water rose from the metal particles, or the more heat energy was developed.

James Prescott Joule was able to refine this system, making it extremely accurate. The unit of work, the joule, is named for him. He was able to find an exact mechanical or work term for heat. The following equations show these relationships for the two common systems of measurement:

4.18 joules = 1 calorie;

778 foot-pounds of work = 1 BRITISH THERMAL UNIT or B.T.U.      M. S.

SEE ALSO: CALORIE; HEAT; JOULE; MACHINES, SIMPLE; POWER; WORK

**Energy conversion** see Energy, Machinery

✳ **THINGS TO DO**

**HOW DOES A STEAM ENGINE WORK?**

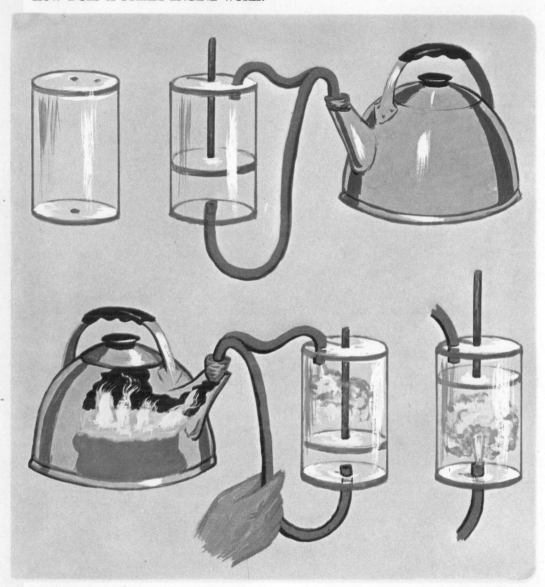

1 Follow the adjoining diagram to assemble a homemade steam engine.
2 Find a tall, clear, heat-resistant plastic container with a cover. Drill a hole in the bottom of the container and one hole off center in the cover.
3 Cut a circle of plastic from a second cover that will fit into the container.
4 Cut slits in the center of the two covers to insert a tongue depressor, or a pencil may be used to act as the piston rod.
5 Insert the ends of two pieces of rubber tubing into a cork which fits snugly in the spout of a teakettle.
6 Boil the water in the kettle. Push the other two ends of the tubes slightly into each opening on the ends of the container.
7 Wearing a glove, alternately pinch one tube at a time to shut off the steam. Alternate the steam intake. This causes the piston rod to move forward and back. If the exposed end of the piston were attached to a crankshaft, work could be done.

# Engine

**Engine** An engine is a machine which changes ENERGY into some form of useful mechanical work. At one time, wind machines (windmills) and water-powered machines (hydraulic turbines) were considered engines. The engine of today, however, refers to the heat or combustion engine. The difference is simply that a heat engine transforms heat, or *thermal,* energy into mechanical work. The other devices depend upon *kinetic,* or "moving," energy (such as blowing wind or falling water) to produce power.

An engine burns or consumes FUEL in order to produce steam or hot gases. The heat energy contained by steam or GAS is released by various mechanical methods to cause a shaft to rotate. Two major classifications of engines are the external and internal combustion engines. These machines function by either a rotating action (turbine) or a reciprocating action (piston).

### EXTERNAL COMBUSTION

External combustion engines use fuel in a unit separate from the power-producing unit. These engines derive their names from the nature of their heat source such as STEAM, solar (sun) and nuclear. Even though there are several heat sources, they all usually transform their thermal energy through steam generation. For this reason, only steam-type engines will be discussed in this section.

*Turbine:* The steam turbine is seldom referred to as an engine, perhaps because of its immense size compared to all other types of engines.

*Reciprocating:* The simplest reciprocating-type steam engine consists of a cylinder, piston, connecting rod, crankshaft and flywheel. Attached to the cylinder is some variation of a valve. Steam generated by a boiler

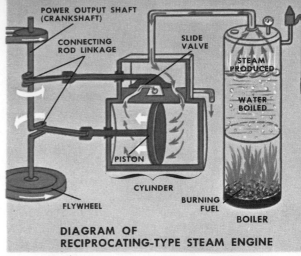

**DIAGRAM OF RECIPROCATING-TYPE STEAM ENGINE**

The early steam engines, though inefficient, opened the way to modern industry

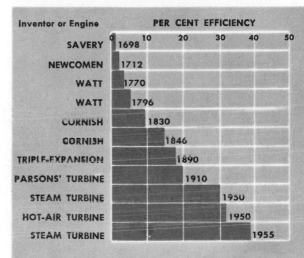

| Inventor or Engine | PER CENT EFFICIENCY |
|---|---|
| SAVERY | 1698 |
| NEWCOMEN | 1712 |
| WATT | 1770 |
| WATT | 1796 |
| CORNISH | 1830 |
| CORNISH | 1846 |
| TRIPLE-EXPANSION | 1890 |
| PARSONS' TURBINE | 1910 |
| STEAM TURBINE | 1950 |
| HOT-AIR TURBINE | 1950 |
| STEAM TURBINE | 1955 |

The giant, triple-flow steam turbine is used to produce great quantities of power

Allis-Chalmers Mfg. Co.

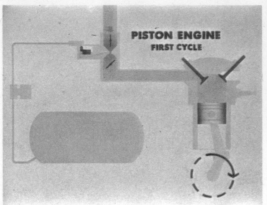

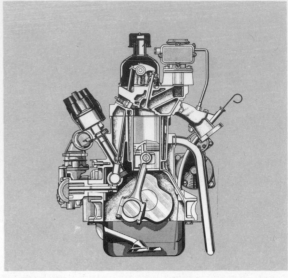

The four cycles of the piston engine (right) are intake, compression, explosion, exhaust

Civil Air Patrol; American Motors

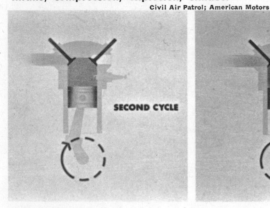

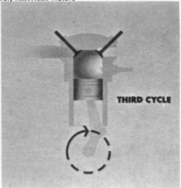

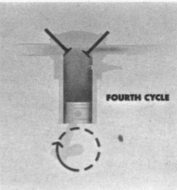

is piped to the valve. The valve, in turn, admits high-pressure steam to either end of the cylinder at the proper instant. As the steam enters the cylinder, it expands in an effort to reduce its pressure back to normal. This expansion produces a large force on the piston which is free to slide in the cylinder. As the piston moves under pressure, the connecting rod linkage turns or cranks the power output shaft (*crankshaft*). The sliding valve moves with the piston, first admitting steam at one end of the cylinder, and then the other. This results in a pushing and pulling motion on the crankshaft. Whatever steam is left is given off through the valve at the end of each stroke.

The heavy flywheel attached to the crankshaft maintains a constant rotary motion, for the reciprocating (back and forth) action can be uneven. The power developed depends upon the pressure and quantity of steam admitted to the cylinder during a specific period of time.

Reciprocating steam engines are classified in several ways:

(1) *by action:* (a) single acting—steam is admitted at one end of the cylinder; (b) double acting—steam is admitted alternately at both ends of the cylinder;

(2) *by direction of piston movement:* (a) horizontal; (b) vertical; (c) inclined;

(3) *by stages of expansion:* (a) double—a larger cylinder further expands steam from the first cylinder; (b) triple—a larger cylinder further expands steam from the second cylinder;

(4) *by steam entry and exhaust position:* (a) counterflow—steam enters and leaves at the same end of the cylinder; (b) uniflow—steam enters at the end, and leaves (exhausts) at the middle of the cylinder.

The valve mechanism is the most critical part of the engine. The maximum power produced depends upon how well the valve admits steam, seals the cylinder during steam expansion, and exhausts the steam. An example was given of the sliding valve used in a simple engine. Lifting type valves are used for very high-temperature steam closures. These are disk-shaped valves which raise and lower from ports in the cylinder head.

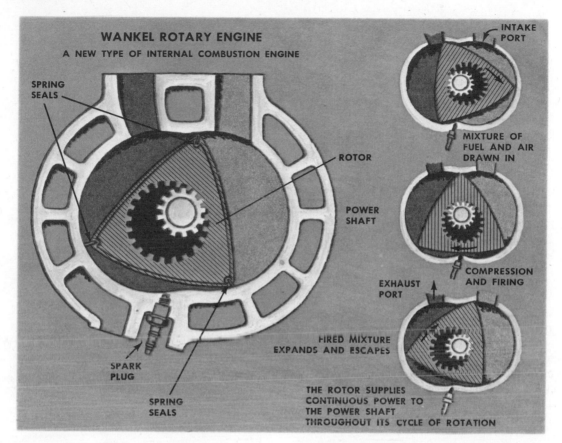

WANKEL ROTARY ENGINE
A NEW TYPE OF INTERNAL COMBUSTION ENGINE

SPRING SEALS

ROTOR

POWER SHAFT

SPARK PLUG

SPRING SEALS

INTAKE PORT

MIXTURE OF FUEL AND AIR DRAWN IN

COMPRESSION AND FIRING

EXHAUST PORT

FIRED MIXTURE EXPANDS AND ESCAPES

THE ROTOR SUPPLIES CONTINUOUS POWER TO THE POWER SHAFT THROUGHOUT ITS CYCLE OF ROTATION

Steam engines have a variable speed and high torque (rotation), characteristics which are most desirable for operation of heavy machinery. Steam engines in locomotives are rapidly giving way to the diesel, while steamship power has been switched from reciprocating engines to turbines. Horsepower ratings of piston-type steam engines do not usually exceed 1000 H.P.

### INTERNAL COMBUSTION

The internal combustion engine differs from the external combustion engine in that the fuel is burned *within* the engine's expansion chamber. The basic operation of internal combustion engines is quite similar to steam engines. There are some modifications due to the different nature of the fuels used. All internal combustion engines have the following characteristic cycle: (a) compress air; (b) raise air temperature by the combustion of fuel at a high pressure; (c) produce work from heated air by expansion back to normal: (d) exhaust gas.

A. *Reciprocating:* Gasoline and diesel engines represent almost all uses of reciprocating internal combustion engines. The major difference between these engines is that the gasoline engine burns fuel at constant *volume,* called the *Otto cycle,* while the diesel burns fuel at constant *pressure,* called the *diesel cycle.*

1. *Gasoline reciprocating engines:* Gasoline piston-type engines are commonly used as power sources for automobiles, trucks, aircraft, boats, lawn mowers and many other powered devices. The smaller utility engines produce as little as one HORSEPOWER, while the larger aircraft engines exceed 3000 horsepower.

Characteristic of the gasoline engine is a *carburetor* for feeding the fuel and mixing it with air outside the combustion chamber; and an *ignition system* for firing the mixture.

Although gasoline engines may assume several different shapes due to the arrangement of cylinders (in a line, "V", horizontally opposed, and radial), they basically function as either a two-stroke cycle or four-stroke cycle engine.

The two-stroke engine requires two strokes of the piston (one revolution of the crankshaft) to complete the combustion cycle, while the four-stroke engine requires four strokes of the piston (two revolutions of the crankshaft) to complete its cycle.

a) *Four-stroke:* On the first stroke down, the air and fuel vapor are admitted to the cylinder by opening the intake valve. During the second stroke, the intake valve closes and compression starts. At the start of the third stroke (the power stroke), an electric discharge from the spark plug ignites the fuel mixture causing a mild explosion. This explosion makes the expanding gases push the piston downward. The fourth stroke completes the cycle by opening the exhaust valve to release the burned gases from the cylinder.

An electric starting motor is commonly used to revolve the crankshaft initially. The intake and exhaust valves are geared to the crankshaft to properly coordinate the instant of opening and closing.

**The four-stroke automotive engine has a power stroke only once in four strokes**

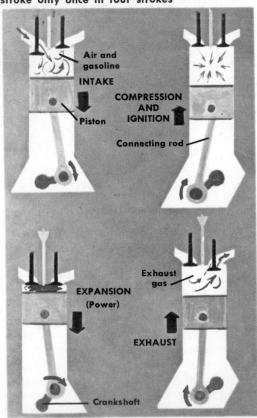

**TWO OF THE STROKES IN A TWO-CYCLE INTERNAL COMBUSTION ENGINE**

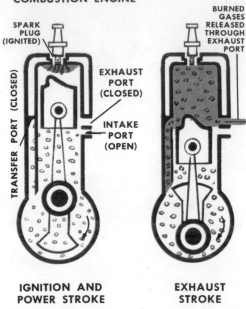

**IGNITION AND POWER STROKE**          **EXHAUST STROKE**

**The two-stroke engine has a power stroke every other stroke**

b) *Two-stroke:* A similar operation takes place in the two-stroke cycle, except the valves are replaced by ports in the cylinder walls which are uncovered as the piston passes by. During the first stroke, the fuel mixture enters the cylinder and is compressed. The fuel mixture is ignited at the start of the second stroke, while the burned gases are exhausted at the end of the stroke.

It would seem logical that since the two-stroke engine has a power stroke twice as often as the four-stroke engine, the power developed by the two-stroke engine would be twice that of the four-stroke engine. But, because of the less efficient operation due to the mixture of burned gases with the combustible fuel, and the loss of unburned fuel through the exhaust port, the two-stroke engine develops only 70–90% more horsepower than the four-stroke engine.

2. *Diesel:* The characteristic difference in operation between the gasoline and diesel engine is that the diesel admits only air during the intake stroke, and the fuel is automatically ignited when forced into the cylinder. The diesel engine, therefore, has no carburetor or ignition system. Fuel injectors supply fuel under high pressure of 1200–3000 pounds per square inch when the air is

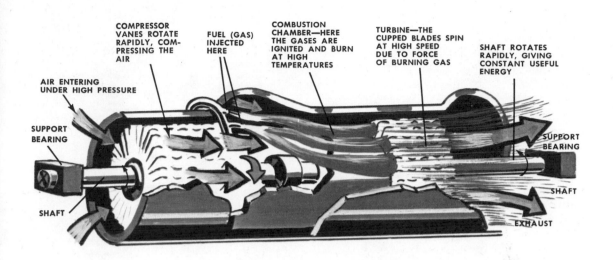

COMPRESSOR
VANES ROTATE
RAPIDLY, COM-
PRESSING THE
AIR

FUEL (GAS)
INJECTED
HERE

COMBUSTION
CHAMBER—HERE
THE GASES ARE
IGNITED AND BURN
AT HIGH
TEMPERATURES

TURBINE—THE
CUPPED BLADES SPIN
AT HIGH SPEED
DUE TO FORCE
OF BURNING GAS

SHAFT ROTATES
RAPIDLY, GIVING
CONSTANT USEFUL
ENERGY

AIR ENTERING
UNDER HIGH PRESSURE

SUPPORT
BEARING

SUPPORT
BEARING

SHAFT

SHAFT

EXHAUST

### SINGLE-SHAFT GAS TURBINE ENGINE

**This type of engine is used in stationary power plants**

**A gas turbine has one main rotating shaft running down its core. The great efficiency of this type of engine is due to the rapid conversion of heat energy to kinetic energy in the turbine. Also, the motion of the shaft is smooth and continuous, rather than "up and down" as in a piston engine. There is no power lost**

compressed to its smallest volume. As the fine spray of fuel thoroughly intermixes with the high-temperature air, combustion occurs. The process of injection, ignition and combustion takes place in only a few thousandths of a second.

The low fuel cost and high thermal efficiency make the diesel practical for power locomotives, trucks and small electrical generating plants. Horsepower usually ranges from 50 to 5000.

B. *Gas turbine:* A simple gas turbine consists of: (a) a rotary compressor unit, (b) a combustion chamber, and (c) a turbine.

The most familiar application of the gas turbine is the *turbojet* (abbreviated "jet") engine used by aircraft. As shown in the illustration, air enters the front opening and is compressed. When it reaches the combustion chamber, it mixes with constantly sprayed and burning fuel. A tremendous heat forms and expands the resulting gases. The heated gases are directed at turbine blades which cause the turbine to rotate 8000–16,000 revolutions per minute. A shaft connected at the turbine drives the compressor at the front end. The gases are

forced out through a nozzle-type opening at high velocity to provide the action-reaction "thrust" required for propulsion. A variation of this application is the turboprop engine. The turbine drives a propeller which produces 80% of the aircraft's power, while the jet provides 20%.

Since horsepower varies with speed, it is not a suitable measure for aircraft power. Instead, *thrust,* measured in pounds, is used:

$$\text{H.P.} = \frac{\text{Thrust (in pounds)} \times \text{Air speed (ft/sec)}}{550}$$

Except for a starter plug, no ignition apparatus is required. No pistons or valves are needed. No engine warm-up periods are necessary because there are few bearings and no metal-to-metal sliding surfaces. Lubrication is simple and the lowest-cost fuels are used. There is little to no vibration and the engine is self-cooling. The horsepower-to-weight ratio is higher than in any other engine, but so is the fuel consumption.

E. I. D.

SEE ALSO: AUTOMOBILE, JET PROPULSION, MOTOR, NUCLEAR ENERGY, ROCKET ENGINES, TURBINE

EGYPTIAN PYRAMIDS

RUINS OF GREEK TEMPLE

MEDIEVAL CASTLE

ANCIENT ENGINEER

HANGING GARDENS OF BABYLON

Through history, engineering scientists have developed different forms and styles for construction

**Engineering** For the past century, engineering has been defined as the art of using natural sources of ENERGY and materials to satisfy the ever-increasing wants of man. Because engineering has become so complex and also better understood, a modern idea of the field is needed. Engineering is the scientific coordination and application of men, money, materials, and scientific methods to the needs of man.

There is a distinct difference between the scientist and the engineer, although engineering is commonly referred to as a scientific profession. The scientist is a discoverer—he engages in "pure" science, the learning and formulation of new ideas, methods and materials. He prepares the results of his work so that it may be used by others for the benefit of man. The engineer, then, is the person who uses these discoveries of fact to analyze the problem logically and to produce something of worth. He may be an inventor, a designer, a specialist or "general practitioner." Engineers have

one common characteristic: they are always looking for a better way—a newer, cheaper, more productive use of materials and energy to constantly improve the standard of living.

### HISTORY

Great engineering marvels have been traced back to Biblical times. The Pyramids of Egypt stand even today, but the Hanging Gardens of Babylon have long since disappeared. The harbors built by the ancient Greeks, and the roads, bridges, aqueducts, and drainage systems constructed by the Romans, are later examples of magnificent engineering achievement. Calling those who originated these projects "engineers" has led to some dispute. Who could say those builders understood the basic reasons for the success of their accomplishments? Some argue that it was not by analysis or by formula that they were able to predict the results, but by trial and error. Nevertheless, modern engineering feats are still rivaled by the skill of past master builders.

GOTHIC CATHEDRAL

UNITED NATIONS BUILDING, NEW YORK

Two main divisions of engineering are noted for historical purposes. The first is the field of *military engineering* which developed ballistics, and war machines such as catapults and wall-scaling devices. As man realized the benefits of military engineering in war, he turned toward peaceful application of the science. Thus out of military engineering grew the second division, *civil engineering*. This field was called "civil" to separate it from military applications.

The modern development of civil engineering began in the 18th century with the construction of canals, roads and bridges—the most outstanding advance since before the Dark Ages. John Smeaton (1724–1792) was the first to be given recognition as a civil engineer. The United States Military Academy at West Point offered the first general engineering course in this country in 1802, while Rensselaer Polytechnic Institute at Troy, New York, offered the first civil engineering degree in 1824. As the need developed for engineers to exchange their ideas, the American Society of Civil Engineers was founded in 1852.

Several inventions in the 19th century complicated the existing field of civil engineering so that it became necessary to branch into different fields. This period of mechanical development, which brought forth the steam engine, the cotton gin, and the spinning jenny, contributed to the beginnings of mechanical engineering; while civil engineering, as it is known today, became involved only with the construction of bridges, roads and buildings. From this period on, engineering grew very rapidly, expanding and specializing in new fields of study as scientific discovery progressed.

### FIELDS OF ENGINEERING

The Engineers' Council for Professional Development (E.C.P.D.), a conference body which establishes the educational and professional standards of engineering, now recognizes engineering degrees awarded in twenty-two fields of specialization. They are as follows:

1) Aeronautical
2) Agricultural
3) Architectural
4) Ceramic
5) Chemical
6) Civil
7) Electrical
8) Engineering mechanics
9) Engineering physics
10) Engineering science
11) General engineering
12) Geological
13) Geophysical
14) Industrial
15) Mechanical
16) Metallurgical
17) Mining
18) Naval architecture and marine
19) Petroleum
20) Sanitary
21) Textile
22) Welding

As will be illustrated later, there are even further refinements of specialized study within these engineering specialties.

The fundamental education of an engineer begins with extensive study in several physical sciences: MATHEMATICS, PHYSICS, CHEMISTRY, and MECHANICS. As he specializes, he draws upon sciences which are the basis of his specialization, such as biology, geology and economics. Engineering courses accredited by the E.C.P.D. require either four or five years of study to obtain an undergraduate degree. An engineer can then continue in studying for a Master's degree (one to two additional years), and then for a Doctor's degree (two years or more beyond a Master's).

Engineering institutions in the United States have increased from 180 in 1949 to 233 in 1959.

At present, approximately 424,000 engineers are practicing their profession in the United States. This total is composed of:

41,500 in chemical engineering
100,000 in civil engineering
107,000 in electrical engineering
101,000 in mechanical and industrial engineering
32,300 in mining and metallurgical engineering
42,300 in all other engineering fields.

In order to define the major engineering fields more precisely, each major specialty needs to be discussed,

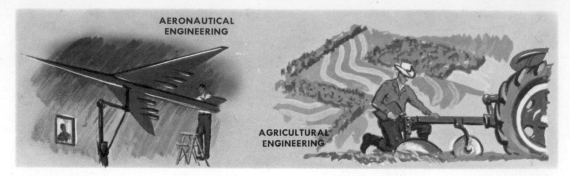

*Aeronautical engineering:* This branch of engineering is concerned with the design, production and maintenance of AIRCRAFT structures and power units. Evolving from the field of mechanical engineering, the aeronautical engineer is considered an engineer of flight. Up until World War II, the aeronautical engineer, a general practitioner in his field, could work on almost any phase of flight known at that time. However, since the advent of missiles, rockets and satellites, he tends to choose a specific field such as aircraft structures, missile structures or jet power plant. Aeronautical engineering has advanced at a tremendous rate since the close of World War II. Aircraft which break the sound barrier are now common. Recent flights of astronauts into outer space reveal that the aeronautical engineer is at the threshold of an expanding field.

*Agricultural engineering:* The agricultural engineer is concerned with the physical problems in the preparation and production of land, and the storage and processing of agricultural products. Specialties include power and machinery, farm structures, processing, and soil and water conservation. It is obvious from this that this engineer must have a thorough working understanding of farms and agriculture in addition to his engineering fundamentals.

*Architectural engineering:* Architectural engineering combines architecture with the structural design aspect of civil engineering for design and construction of buildings. An architect is concerned primarily with the appearance of his design, while the civil engineer regards structural soundness as his objective. By uniting the two fields, functional structures can be erected at a minimum cost. Structural, mechanical, and electrical systems are coordinated by the architectural engineer in all phases of building construction. Perhaps the most notable example of architectural engineering is the Empire State Building in New York City, the tallest structure in the world.

*Ceramic engineering:* The ceramic engineer is concerned with the design and production of products made from nonmetallic, inorganic sands or clays. In addition to solving problems of brick, tile, and glass production, the ceramic engineer helps the electrical engineer with insulator problems and the missile engineer with heat and friction problems. Together with metallurgical engineers, the ceramic engineers developed a ceramic and metal mixture, called *cermet* which is superior to either individual ingredient for specific applications.

*Chemical engineering:* Using CHEMISTRY as his "pure science" foundation, the chemi-

ELECTRICAL ENGINEERING

CIVIL ENGINEERING

cal engineer is most concerned with manufacturing processes where materials are changed in state, energy content, or composition. For example, chemical engineers devise the necessary equipment and methods for making rayon, nylon, explosives, drugs, petroleum products, plastics, and chemicals —to mention only a few. He may also work in the laboratory controlling the operations and testing the products. While the chemist researches for new materials, the chemical engineer looks for ways to produce the materials quickly and cheaply.

*Civil engineering:* Civil engineers plan the design, construction, and maintenance of both fixed structures and ground transportation facilities. This field is perhaps the broadest of all since many specialties have evolved from it, such as structural, highway, dam, city planning, and hydraulic engineering. Leading modern accomplishments of the civil engineer are the Panama Canal, the Hoover and Grand Coulee dams, the George Washington and Golden Gate bridges.

*Electrical engineering:* This branch of engineering deals with problems of ELECTRICITY and magnetism. The electrical engineer designs and tests generators, motors, transformers, and electrical appliances. He may be responsible for the installation of power lines. From this field has evolved the elec-

tronics, radio, television and signal engineer. The greatest accomplishments of this branch have been made in the area of ELECTRONICS, as illustrated by the development of television, high-speed computers, and control devices for industry and the military.

*Industrial engineering:* Industrial engineering is concerned with the design, improvement and installation of combined systems of men, materials and equipment. This field is often thought of as management engineering for it covers a broad area of every manufacturing activity. The industrial engineer is involved with design, specification and evaluation of plant layouts, materials handling systems, methods analyses, wage systems, work measurement, and management operations in order to promote the most efficient organization practicable.

*Mechanical engineering:* This field treats the design, manufacture, and operation of machinery, engines and tools; and heating, refrigeration and, ventilating equipment. The field is so broad that the engineer often specializes as a machine design, automotive, marine, power plant or heating and ventilating engineer. Most inventions have originated in the field of mechanical engineering. Manufacturers depend heavily upon the mechanical engineers to provide the basic needs for their engineering requirements.

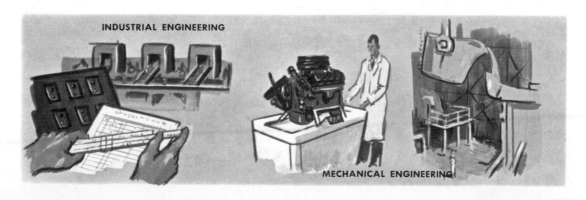

INDUSTRIAL ENGINEERING

MECHANICAL ENGINEERING

SANITARY ENGINEERING

MINING ENGINEERING

WELDING ENGINEERING

TEXTILE ENGINEERING

MARINE ENGINEERING

*Metallurgical engineering:* The metallurgical engineer is interested in the practical use of the properties of METALS and their AL-LOYS. He is involved in problems of extracting metals from their ores and of metal refining. The art of welding and heat treating are important advances in this field. The metallurgical engineer's specialized knowledge of metal characteristics has been important in enabling the United States to probe outer space successfully.

*Mining engineering:* This branch includes the location, design, and operation of mineral extractions from the earth. Prospecting for mine locations involves unique underground surveying. Ore transporting and handling techniques have become major engineering specialties within this field. Other allied engineering fields have developed directly or indirectly, such as petroleum, geological and geophysical engineering. The geological (earth crust study) and geophysical (earth subsurface study) engineers get their science background from geology.

*Naval architecture and marine engineering:* Originally, this field was concerned with the structural design and construction of ships, but now it includes all phases of power plant, propulsion, and control system applications as well. The most recent and significant achievement in this field is the use of nuclear reactors to power submarines and surface vessels.

*Sanitary engineering:* As an outgrowth of the civil engineering field, the sanitary engineer's primary interest is that of protecting public health. He is responsible for conceiving, designing, appraising, directing and managing public health works and projects. Such projects include the treatment and distribution of water supplies; the collection, treatment and disposal of sewage; the control of water pollution; rodent control; food control; and air pollution. Sanitary engineering is an extremely important function in large cities where there is dense population.

*Textile engineering:* The textile engineer is to the textile industry as the agricultural engineer is to farming. He is an industrial specialist concerned with the numerous problems of manufacturing cloth and other fabrics.

*Welding engineering:* The welding engineer is a specialist in methods of joining metals. He must have a thorough background in metallurgy so that he can design welding systems and work out techniques that are sound and practical.     E. I. D.

**English Channel** see Europe

**Entomology** (enn-tuh-MAHL-uh-jee) Entomology is the science which deals with all phases of insect study, including the classification of insects. Classification is complex because there are thousands of kinds of insects. The effect of insects on AGRICULTURE is also studied.

SEE: ANIMALS, CLASSIFICATION OF; INSECTA

**Environment** (enn-VYE-run-muhnt) Environment is the sum total of the conditions, influences and material factors surrounding an organism. The external environment includes all living things, and all nonliving things outside the organism. Internal environment is the organization inside the body.

SEE: BALANCE OF NATURE, ECOLOGY, ECO-SYSTEM

**Enzyme** (ENN-zyme) Enzymes are chemical substances made by plants and animals. They are found in all living cells. These substances speed up certain chemical reactions in the cells without being changed themselves by the reactions. Because of this behavior, they are chemical CATALYSTS. A still better description for them is *organic* catalysts, because they are formed by living cells or organisms. Enzymes are necessary to life. The chemical reactions that create life could not take place without the presence of enzymes.

There are many enzymes in the body. Some of them are made entirely of PROTEIN, while others are made of protein combined with certain metals, such as copper, zinc and iron. Enzymes can by destroyed by heat. Some can be activated by light rays, while others are inhibited by them. Substances upon which enzymes act are called *substrates*.

Some enzymes, such as *pepsin,* can act only in an acid medium, while others, such as *trypsin,* can act only in an alkaline (basic) medium. Enzymes may be grouped according to their ability (1) to hasten either the building up of complex compounds from less complex materials (*synthesis*) or (2) to hasten the breaking down of complex compounds into simpler substances (DECOMPOSITION). Each enzyme is specific in its action. For instance, pepsin acts only upon proteins while *amylase* acts only upon STARCHES.

For centuries people have been aware of chemical reactions such as the souring of milk, the changing of sugar into alcohol, and the formation of ammonia from URINE. Later these reactions were found to be caused by the presence of certain microorganisms. The term *ferment* was first used to describe these chemical changes. It was later found that the microorganisms produced specific chemicals—enzymes—that catalyzed definite chemical changes.

Although enzymes are present in all living cells, man is most familiar with those affecting the digestion of foods. *Ptyalin* is present in the SALIVA in the mouth. It breaks down starches into less complex substances

## ✳ THINGS TO DO

### WHAT DO THE ENZYMES DO IN THE STOMACH?

1   Break an egg and separate the yellow from the white. Pour just the white part of the egg into a test tube.
2   Hold the tube over a flame until the white is cooked. Mark the level of the egg in the test tube.
3   Lay it in a pan of water to which pepsin has been added.
4   After one day observe the results. Now carefully add a few drops of dilute hydrochloric acid to the water and pepsin solution.
5   Let it stand for a second day and observe the change.
6   Pepsin is an enzyme in the stomach that breaks down proteins into simpler materials. However, it is not effective unless hydrochloric acid is present.
7   The other enzyme in the stomach, rennin, may be added to a cup of milk. It curds the milk and prepares it for the action of other enzymes.

such as maltose. In the stomach, protein substances are acted upon by hydrochloric acid and then through the enzyme pepsin are transformed into less complex substances, such as *proteoses* and *peptones*. The action of the enzyme pepsin ceases after the partly digested food (*chyme*) leaves the intestine. In the small intestine the proteins which have escaped the action of pepsin will be acted upon by an enzyme called *trypsin*

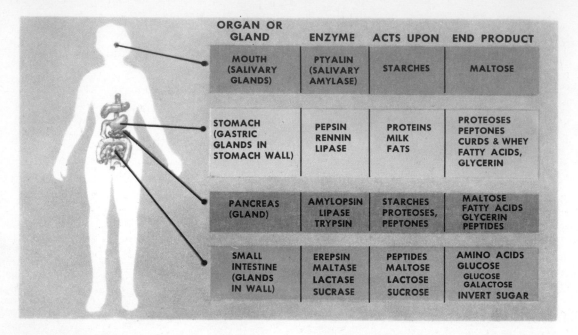

| ORGAN OR GLAND | ENZYME | ACTS UPON | END PRODUCT |
|---|---|---|---|
| MOUTH (SALIVARY GLANDS) | PTYALIN (SALIVARY AMYLASE) | STARCHES | MALTOSE |
| STOMACH (GASTRIC GLANDS IN STOMACH WALL) | PEPSIN RENNIN LIPASE | PROTEINS MILK FATS | PROTEOSES PEPTONES CURDS & WHEY FATTY ACIDS, GLYCERIN |
| PANCREAS (GLAND) | AMYLOPSIN LIPASE TRYPSIN | STARCHES PROTEOSES, PEPTONES | MALTOSE FATTY ACIDS GLYCERIN PEPTIDES |
| SMALL INTESTINE (GLANDS IN WALL) | EREPSIN MALTASE LACTASE SUCRASE | PEPTIDES MALTOSE LACTOSE SUCROSE | AMINO ACIDS GLUCOSE GLUCOSE GALACTOSE INVERT SUGAR |

which is produced by the PANCREAS. Trypsin also acts upon proteose and peptone and transforms them into simpler substances called *peptides*. The final stage in the digestion of proteins is the action of *erepsin* upon them with transformation into the individual AMINO ACIDS which are ready to be absorbed into the bloodstream.

In the small intestine there is an enzyme called *amylase* which is much more potent than ptyalin, though it has the same action as ptyalin on starches and transforms them into maltose. There is an enzyme called *maltase* which changes maltose into glucose. Glucose is the simplest form of sugar. It is ready to be absorbed into the bloodstream just as are the amino acids of proteins.

In the stomach the enzyme *lypase* acts upon fatty substances but is rather weak. In the small intestine, the pancreatic lypase will have a final action upon fats and transform them into FATTY ACIDS and glycerol. The enzyme *rennin* coagulates milk in the stomach and forms a semisolid material called *curd* and a fluid called *whey*. This enzyme is used in the making of cheese. Rennin can be extracted from the stomachs of cows. The enzymes which were discovered first are still called ptyalin, pepsin, rennin, trypsin and amylopsin. However, through agreement of scientists, it is a practice to name an enzyme by adding the suffix *ase* to the name of its substrate (the substance acted upon). For example, lypase acts

upon fat, called in Greek, *lypos*. Proteinase acts upon proteins.

GENES, which set the pattern of HEREDITY of each organism, are believed to act by producing certain enzymes. The set of enzymes an organism has determines the chemical reactions that will take place in the organism and so determines the physiology and structure of the organism. G. A. D.
SEE ALSO: DIGESTIVE SYSTEM, ORGANIC COMPOUNDS, SUGARS

**Eocene** see Cenozoic Era, Geologic time table

**Epidemic** An epidemic is the sudden occurrence of an unusual number of cases of a contagious DISEASE in a community. Health officials keep records of reported cases of contagious diseases by day, week, month, and year. By comparison of such recorded data, health officers have an idea of the behavior of a contagious disease in a community. When the number of cases of a contagious disease is unusually high in comparison with the previous years, an epidemic exists. If several cases of a disease occur almost at the same time, it could be that they have a common source.

There are ways to detect the source of an epidemic. One way is to note the *incubation period* (the lapse of time between exposure to a disease and the first occurrence of symptoms). Health officers try to locate the source of a disease in an attempt to control the spread of it. They also must understand how contagious diseases are spread. Some are spread by coughing, by kissing, or by contaminating the water supply by feces.

Epidemics occur in spurts. MEASLES can be used as an example of the mechanism of an epidemic. In a given population many susceptible persons can develop measles. The rate can be so high that almost everyone in a certain age range becomes affected. After recovery from the attack, these patients become immune. The disease appears to die out temporarily in the community until a new generation of unprotected persons is born. Then, should an outsider bring a case to the community, a certain peak in the number of cases of measles would appear which again could reach epidemic proportions.      G. A. D.

SEE ALSO: BLACK PLAGUE, MEDICINE

**Epidermis** see Skin

**Epiglottis** see Respiratory system

**Epilepsy** (EPP-uh-lepp-see) Epilepsy is a disease of the NERVOUS SYSTEM. It most commonly shows itself in sudden attacks of unconsciousness. No characteristic structural defect or injury of the BRAIN is found in all epileptics. In about 20% of all patients no brain change at all is detected.

Along with unconsciousness, there are convulsive contractions of certain groups of muscles, which quickly spread to the whole body. These seizures are frequently preceded by certain sensations of the body so that the patient knows an attack is coming. The sensations, called the *aura,* vary widely. They may be a griping sensation in the abdomen, or an excessive flow of saliva, or even a series of odd thoughts running through the mind. The aura, as established by the individual patient, is repeated before each attack.

Among the first group of muscles to begin their intermittent contractions are those of the jaws. The patient froths at the mouth; the tongue may protrude and get in the way of the teeth during biting motions. One of the first steps to prevent the patient from harming himself is to put a piece of wood or a similar object between his jaws, thus protecting the tongue.

There are three types of epilepsy. The severe type described above is called *grand mal;* a secondary, less severe type is called *petit mal.* The third type is more inclined to changes in the mental activities. The patient does not lose consciousness, but there is a period of loss of memory lasting from a few minutes to several hours.

Between the attacks of all forms of epilepsy the patient is perfectly normal. He can do his customary work and sometimes exhibits exceptional brilliance. Napoleon Bonaparte, Mohammed, Peter the Great, Julius Caesar—some certain victims of the disease—are examples of those with well-developed mental faculties.      H. K. S.

SEE ALSO: CONVULSION, ELECTROENCEPHALOGRAPH

**Epinephrine** see Adrenalin

**Epiphyte** (EPP-uh-fyte) An epiphyte is a PLANT which grows attached to another plant. It derives no food from its host, only support and better light conditions. Its roots take water and minerals from the air, and the decayed matter found on its host plant.

SEE: ORCHID, PARASITE

**Many orchids and members of the pineapple family, including Spanish moss, are epiphytes**

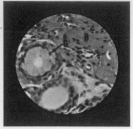

Epithelial tissue (B) surrounds the glands (G) of the trachea. The top cells are flat (squamous) and there are several layers. The tissue is called *stratified squamous epithelium*

Photo-micrograph by National Teaching Aids, Inc.

**Epithelial tissue** (epp-uh-THEE-lee-uhl) Epithelial tissue covers and protects the body surfaces and cavities. The SKIN, the digestive canal, the LUNGS, the urinary system, the glands, and the blood vessels are all lined with epithelial tissue. In addition to covering and protecting, epithelial tissue keeps water and salts from escaping from the body. It forms part of sense organs and glands. Epithelial tissue can secrete fluids and chemicals, and can absorb nourishment.

Epithelial tissues are made up of one or more layers of closely-packed cells. There are three main types: flat, cuboidal, and columnar. The flat thin cells, forming *squamous tissue,* usually act as a protective covering as in the outer layers of the skin. The square cells of *cuboidal tissue* are found lining ducts in the THYROID and KIDNEY. The tall, narrow cells of *columnar tissue,* lining the intestines, secrete and absorb. Columnar cells often have fine protoplasmic projections called *cilia.*

With few exceptions, epithelial tissue contains no blood vessels. The cells are held together, and to the surface on which they rest, by a small amount of intercellular material.                E. M. S.

SEE ALSO: CONNECTIVE TISSUE, HISTOLOGY, TISSUE

**Epoch** (EPP-uhk) In geology, an epoch is a subdivision, or part, of a geologic period of time. The period is, in turn, part of a geologic era. For example, the CENOZOIC ERA is divided into two periods. The first of these, the Quaternary period, is divided into two epochs—Pleistocene and Recent.

SEE: GEOLOGIC TIME TABLE

**Equation** An equation in MATHEMATICS asks a question or makes an assertion. An equation can usually be identified by the presence of an equal sign ($=$). The equation $x + 2 = 6$ asks: "Is there a number such that when 2 is added to it, the sum will be 6?" The answer is: "Yes. The number 4."

The equation $x + 3 = x$ asks: "Is there a number such that when 3 is added to it the number remains unchanged?" The answer is: "No. There is no such number."

An equation which asks a question is called a *conditional equation.*

An equation of the form
$$X + 1 = 1 + X$$
does not ask a question. It asserts that for any number $X$, $X + 1 = 1 + X$. This type of an equation is called an *identity.*
                                            I. K. F.

SEE ALSO: ALGEBRA, ARITHMETIC

**Equator** (ih-KWAY-ter) The equator is an imaginary circle around the middle of the EARTH. It is equally distant from both the North and South Poles. It is the dividing line between the Northern Hemisphere and the Southern Hemisphere.

In ASTRONOMY, the celestial equator is an imaginary circle in the sky formed where the celestial sphere would be crossed by a line drawn up from Earth's equator.

The equator divides Earth into two parts

Courtesy Society For Visual Education, Inc.

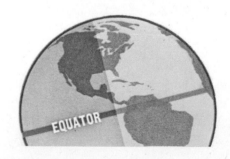

---

✳ **THINGS TO DO**

### ESTABLISHING PHYSICAL EQUILIBRIUM

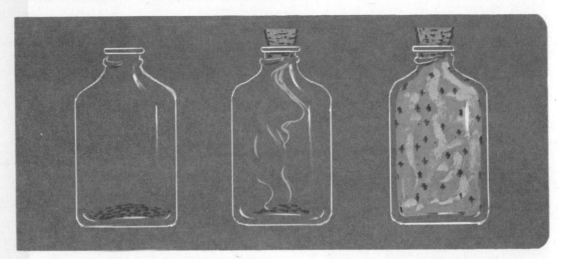

1. Place some iodine crystals in a bottle. Stopper the bottle.
2. After a short period, some of the iodine evaporates and the bottle fills with a purple gas. Later, the color of the gas no longer changes.
3. What has happened is that a particle of iodine, an iodine molecule, has escaped to the gas phase, and one of the gaseous molecules has collided with the solid material and stuck. Even though there is a change, one can not observe this change. When the number of molecules escaping the surface equals the number of molecules striking the surface and sticking, equilibrium is established.

**J.R.S.**

---

**Equilibrium** (ee-kwuh-LIBB-ree-um) Most chemical reactions do not proceed very rapidly, nor do they reach completion. When two reactions occur in such a way that their rates are equal but their effects are opposite, it may seem that the reaction has stopped. When this happens, a state of equilibrium has been reached.

Physical equilibrium can be similarly defined. Two or more forces may act on an object in such a way that the forces balance each other and leave the object unmoved. A state of equilibrium then exists.

If a rubber ball is dropped into a pond of water, it floats. A state of equilibrium exists. The forces pushing downward on the ball are equal to the forces pushing upward.

Equilibrium in living organisms refers to the state of balance maintained by living things in relation to the earth's GRAVITY. All animals have a center of gravity. This center in animals with appendages may be some distance from, or well above, the base of the animals. The earthworm has little trouble keeping its equilibrium, while the giraffe needs several sensory receptors to help it keep its body position in relation to its environment.

In vertebrates the sense receptors are the eyes, the semicircular canals in the labyrinth of the ears, muscle spindles, and the sympathetic nerve endings in the abdominal organs. All these receptors send messages to the brain to indicate the position of the body in relation to the center of the earth.

J. R. S.

SEE ALSO: BUOYANCY, EAR, HOMEOSTASIS

**Equilibrium of forces** see Forces

On about March 21 and September 21, neither pole tilts toward the sun. These days are called *equinoxes*

On about December 21 (winter solstice), the North Pole slants farthest away from the sun and receives minimum heat

All pictures courtesy Society For Visual Education, Inc.

On about June 21 (summer solstice), the North Pole slants most toward the sun and receives maximum heat

**Equinox** During the winter season there are more hours of darkness than of light in each 24 hours. During the summer there are more hours of light than of darkness in each 24 hours. Twice each year there are days with equal hours of light and darkness. These days of equal light and dark occur at the time of year called the equinox. The word *equinox* means "equal night."

One equinox occurs about March 21. This is called the spring or *vernal equinox*. The other equinox occurs about September 21

and is called the *autumnal equinox*. In the Northern Hemisphere the period from the vernal to the autumnal equinox contains the SEASONS spring and summer. From the autumnal to the vernal equinox are autumn and winter in the Northern Hemisphere.

The earth rotates on its axis at a fixed angle—23½°—to the axis of the sun's rotation. This is called the *angle of the ecliptic*. Only twice a year, at the equinoxes, are the sun's rays directly overhead at the equator. During the rest of the year, the days and nights are unequal, and the sun appears a little to the north or the south instead of directly overhead.                J. D. B.

SEE ALSO: DAY AND NIGHT, EARTH

**Era** (IRR-uh) In geology, an era is a major division of geologic time. The five geologic eras are the ARCHEOZOIC ERA, the PROTEROZOIC ERA, the PALEOZOIC ERA, the MESOZOIC ERA, and the CENOZOIC ERA.

SEE: GEOLOGIC TIME TABLE

**Erbium** Erbium is one of the RARE-EARTH metallic elements. Carl G. Mosander discovered it in 1843. It appears in minerals often found in veins of granite or pegmatite. Erbium is dark gray in color.

Erbium (symbol Er) can be obtained by crystallization of its bromates, occurring when they are cooled below 2800°F. Its commonest oxide is rose-red, formula $Er_2O_3$. Erbium also forms many other colored compounds. Metallic erbium has interesting anti-magnetic properties at low temperatures. Its atomic number is 68; its atomic weight is 167.26 (167.27, O = 16); and its specific gravity is 4.77.                D. E. Z.

SEE ALSO: ATOM, ELEMENTS

**Erg** An erg (abbreviated e) is a unit of WORK or energy equal to the work done by a force of one DYNE when it causes the object to which the force is applied to move one centimeter in the direction of the applied force.

SEE: FORCES, MEASUREMENT

**Ermine** see Weasel

---

✳ **THINGS TO DO**

HOW CAN GRAIN FARMERS SAVE THEIR TOPSOIL?

**Materials:** 3 large aluminum foil cake pans, rubber tubing, clay, soil and sand mixture, topsoil, cereal grain, dishes

1  Cut a hole near the top rim on one side of each pan. Tape a piece of rubber tube to each hole.

2  Put layers of clay, soil, and sand mixture in each. Add a top layer of rich topsoil.

3  Rest one end of each pan on a block of wood to elevate it at a 30 degree angle. The hose on the opposite end should be directed into a dish to collect the water.

4  In one pan make rows across the width of the pan and plant a cereal grain—wheat, oats, or barley.

5  In the second pan make rows the length of the pan and plant the same cereal grain.

6  Do not plant anything in the third field.

7  With a sprinkling can pour the same amount of water (rain) over each pan.

8  What happens to the topsoil in each case? Measure the amount of soil that leaves the tube and settles in the collecting dishes.

9  The first field illustrates contour farming where the farmer sows the seeds around a hill. In the second field the rows go up and down the hill. This prevents more soil erosion than the third field but is not as efficient as the first method.

**Erosion** Erosion is the wearing away of land by the action of water, gravity and wind. Snow, ice, rain, frosts, floods, and tidal waves take away the good topsoil and leave the land bare. When the topsoil is gone, plants and trees cannot live, and gullies and dust bowls are formed.

Moving water carries loose particles of soil and earth along with it. This sediment, usually valuable topsoil, is carried into small streams, then into rivers, and then out into the ocean. When rushing water follows the same path often enough, it forms a *gully*. The Grand Canyon is a dramatic example of erosion.

Soil erosion is one of the nation's major agricultural problems. It can be remedied by conservation of existing forests and careful reforestation on hills and mountain slopes. The sowing of GRASSES helps form sod which will hold the soil so it cannot be washed away in heavy rains. Farmers are being educated in soil conservation practices, and many plant their fields along the contour of the land.

**Mesas and buttes (small mesas) are upland areas that have eroded**

Courtesy Society For Visual Education, Inc.

All pictures courtesy Society For Visual Education, Inc.

The Grand Canyon was eroded by the Colorado River millions of years ago

Coastal areas are made rough by wave action

Wind and rain can wear off all topsoil

Contour plowing of fields can prevent erosion

Coastal erosion is brought about by the beating of waves against the shore. The waves undermine cliffs and other coastal areas until they break off and drop into the sea. Sea walls help prevent this.    M. R. L.

SEE ALSO: CONSERVATION OF NATURE, GEOLOGY, WEATHERING

**Erythrocyte** see Blood

**Escarpment** (ess-KARP-muhnt) Escarpment is a geological term describing a long line of steep cliffs made by faulting or EROSION. A *fault-scarp* is due to FAULTING. A *cuesta* is the name for an escarpment caused by erosion.

SEE: GEOLOGY, MOUNTAINS

**Esophagus** see Digestive system

A dramatic example of an escarpment

Courtesy Society For Visual Education, Inc.

**Essential oils** Essential oils are the volatile, odorous, usually liquid substances found in certain plants which give odor and flavor to those plants. TURPENTINE is one example. Other essential oils give odor and flavor to consumer goods like PERFUME and chewing gum.

SEE: RESIN

**Ester** An ester is an organic chemical compound formed by the reaction between an acid and an ALCOHOL. In this reaction, the hydrogen of the acid is replaced by carbon from the alcohol, and a molecule of water is formed.

SEE: ACIDS AND BASES, FAT, ORGANIC COMPOUND, SOAP

**Estivation** (ess-tuh-VAY-shun) Estivation describes an almost completely quiet state which a plant or animal goes through to adapt itself to abnormally dry or hot living conditions. The organism withdraws to a cooler, wetter place, or its METABOLISM slows, or both.

SEE: HIBERNATION

**Estrogen** (ESS-truh-junn) Estrogen is a female hormone. Its action changes a young girl into a woman. It is made by the OVARY, ADRENAL GLAND, and placenta. The TESTIS of the male also contains a certain amount of estrogen.

There are three natural estrogens— estriol, estrone, and estradiol. They are all chemicals belonging to the group called *steroids*. They affect the secondary sex characteristics (voice, hair growth, muscle and bone structure, fat deposits, and also the personality) in the females of mammals. The role of estrogens and other hormones secreted following fertilization of the egg is to prepare the uterus to nourish the embryo.
B. J. C.
SEE ALSO: ANDROGEN, ESTROUS CYCLE, MENSTRUATION, STEROID

**Estrous cycle** (ESS-truss) The estrous cycle is part of the reproductive function in mammals. It is the period between the release of one EGG from the ovary and the release of the next egg. In the human female, this period is about 30 days. There are many changes which occur in the ovary, uterus and vagina. This is to prepare for the release of the egg (ovulation).

The PITUITARY plays an important part in the control of the estrous cycle. At the beginning of the cycle, FSH *(follicle stimulating hormone)* is sent out from the pituitary. It influences an egg in the ovary to develop within a casing of cells called a *follicle*. As the follicle ripens, it manufactures estrogens and releases them into the blood stream. ESTROGEN stimulates the pituitary to form and release a second hormone, LH *(luteinizing hormone)*. LH causes the egg to rupture from the follicle and escape from the ovary into the *Fallopian tube*. From the Fallopian tube, the egg descends gradually into the uterus.

Meanwhile, in the ovary the ruptured follicle starts to secrete *progesterone*. This hormone prepares the lining of the uterus for the arrival of the egg. If the egg is not fertilized, the uterine lining sloughs off, and menstruation occurs. The level of progesterone falls, causing the pituitary to send out FSH. This is the signal for a new follicle to begin the development of an egg for the next cycle.

In mammals the number of cycles per year varies considerably. Bats, deer, and others have only one cycle a year. Some rodents ovulate weekly; horses and cows are seasonal; and dogs usually have two cycles a year.
B. J. C.
SEE ALSO: MAMMALIA, MENSTRUATION, OVULATION, REPRODUCTIVE SYSTEM

**Estuary** (ESS-choo-air-ee) An estuary is a funnel-shaped BAY formed when the sea invades a river valley at the point where the RIVER empties. It happens only where the shoreline is sinking or depressed.

SEE: GEOLOGY

**Ether** Diethyl ether, known simply as *ether,* is the most important member of a whole series of ORGANIC COMPOUNDS called *ethers*. Ether is an ANESTHETIC or pain killer. When a person breathes ether he loses consciousness. It is no longer as widely used as formerly because it sometimes causes serious illnesses.

Ether is an excellent SOLVENT for many organic compounds. It is employed in industry and laboratories in this way.

Diethyl ether is prepared from ethyl ALCOHOL, grain alcohol, by mixing it with sulfuric acid. Since ether evaporates rapidly and the vapor forms an explosive mixture with air, ether must be kept away from fire.

J. R. S.

**ETHYL—PISTON RUNS SMOOTHLY**  **NON-ETHYL—"KNOCK" IN PISTON CHAMBER**

Ethyl eliminates "knock" by preventing gasoline vapors from exploding at the wrong time

**Ethyl** "Ethyl gas" is the common name given to automobile and aviation gasolines to which certain substances have been added. These substances are called *additives*. The additives allow the gasoline to be compressed more within the ENGINE than it would without them. This greater compression results in more power and better engine efficiency by eliminating or reducing the kick back or "knock." Knock is experienced when the gasoline vapors are exploded too soon during the engine cycle.

In 1924, *tetraethyl lead,* $Pb(C_2H_5)_4$, came to be used as an additive in "antiknock" gasolines. But since COMBUSTION of gasoline containing only this additive produces lead deposits along the cylinders, other additives were put in. To prevent lead deposits from harming the spark plugs and valves, ethylene dibromide ($C_2H_4Br_2$) and ethylene dichloride ($C_2H_4Cl_2$) were added. The bromine and chlorine react with the lead and escape in the exhaust gases.

Ethyl is also a *radical,* or group, ($C_2H_5$) obtained from ethane ($C_2H_6$) and is the basis for numerous ORGANIC COMPOUNDS. The ethyl group and HYDROXYL group (OH) comprise ethyl ALCOHOL ($C_2H_5OH$). Tetraethyl lead illustrates four ethyl radicals in one compound.

D. L. D.

SEE ALSO: AUTOMOBILE, FUEL, HYDROCARBON, RADICAL

**Ethyl alcohol** see Alcohol

**Ethylene** Ethylene is a colorless gas. It burns easily, giving a bright flame. It is used as an ANESTHETIC, as a blowtorch FUEL, and as an ingredient in certain plastics and polymers.

The formula of ethylene is $C_2H_4$. It is the first member of an organic chemical series, the *olefins,* all of which have the same general formula, $C_nH_{2n}$, and all of which possess two neighboring carbon atoms with a double bond (or two pairs of electrons) between them. They are said to be *unsaturated* carbon atoms—(as in the unsaturated fats.)

Ethylene is made by the pressure-and-catalysis or "cracking" of the saturated gases, PROPANE or ethane. Some useful derived compounds that start with ethylene are: ethylene glycol, an ANTIFREEZE and artificial ripener of fruits; ethylene dibromide, $C_2H_4Br_2$, used in antiknock (or "ETHYL") gasolines; and the poisonous mustard gas $[(C_2H_4Cl)_2S]$.

D. L. D.

SEE ALSO: ORGANIC COMPOUNDS

**Ethylene glycol** see Organic compounds

**Eucalyptus** (yoo-kuh-LIPP-tuhs) Next to the redwood, the eucalyptus is the tallest living thing. It sometimes reaches 300 feet in height. It is an evergreen tree of the myrtle family and is sometimes called the GUM TREE.

The eucalyptus is native to Australia and is also grown in Florida and California. The broad leaves are bluish or green-gray. The

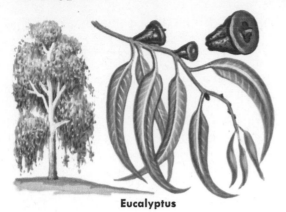

**Eucalyptus**

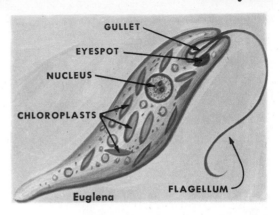

GULLET
EYESPOT
NUCLEUS
CHLOROPLASTS
FLAGELLUM

**Euglena**

rose to white flowers contain honey. The wood has a strong oil odor which insects avoid. It has a spreading root system.

Eucalyptus leaves are dried and an oil is extracted. It is used medicinally for nose and throat trouble and for treating fevers. The oil is almost colorless and has a pungent odor.  H. J. C.

**Eugenics** see Biology; Galton, Sir Francis

**Euglena** (you-GLEE-nuh) Euglena is a tiny, one-celled plant or animal. It is a PLANT since it contains CHLOROPHYLL and can make its own food. It is also usually classed as an ANIMAL since it moves quickly and has an opening for taking in food.

Euglenas are cigar-shaped and measure about one millimeter in length. They are able to move rapidly through the water by means of a squirming, worm-like movement of their bodies and by use of *flagella,* which are whip-like projections at one end of the body.

In structure, the euglena's body is similar to that of other one-celled organisms. The distinction between one-celled animals and one-celled plants is very slight. The euglena is classified as a plant because of its ability to synthesize sugar when exposed to light. Green chloroplasts are present in the body, and thus enable PHOTOSYNTHESIS to take place. Because a euglena has a mouth (*cytostome*), gullet (*cytopharynx*), and moves by means of a flagellum, it is also classified as an animal. In spite of the presence of a mouth and gullet, most of its non-photosynthetic food is absorbed through the body wall from the water in which it lives.

The thin, outer covering of the euglena's body is called the *pellicle.* This surrounds a clear substance called *ectoplasm,* which in turn, surrounds the *endoplasm.* Respiration and excretion are also carried on by means of DIFFUSION through the body wall. Reproduction is by means of longitudinal cell division.

Although the euglena has no true eye, it has an eyespot which is sensitive to light. It will swim toward light.

Euglenas are members of the Phylum PROTOZOA. They are sometimes called *green algae.*  I. H. S.
SEE ALSO: ALGAE

**Euonymus** (yoo-AHN-ih-muss) Euonymus is the name of certain shrubs or small trees used frequently in hedges or borders. They produce clusters of greenish-white flowers. The bark is gray in color and has a smooth surface. The fruit, when ripe, can be recognized by its bright orange-colored seed which is seen as the maturing fruit splits.

The *spindle tree,* found in the eastern part of the United States, is an example of the euonymus. Other varieties found in the U.S. include the strawberry bush, creeping strawberry bush, wahoo and western wahoo. One kind of climbing evergreen is used ornamentally on walls.  D. J. I.

**Two kinds of euonymus**

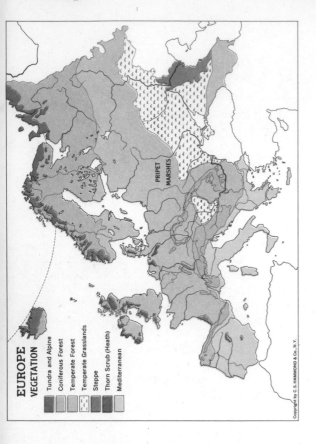

EUROPE VEGETATION

Tundra and Alpine
Coniferous Forest
Temperate Forest
Temperate Grasslands
Steppe
Thorn Scrub (Heath)
Mediterranean

PRIPET MARSHES

Copyright by C. S. HAMMOND & Co., N.Y.

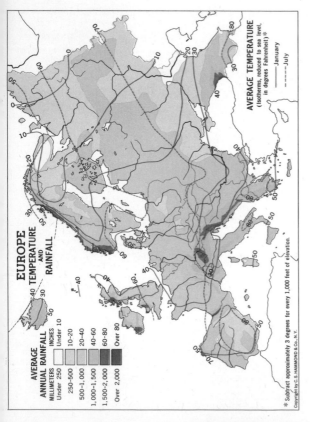

EUROPE TEMPERATURE AND RAINFALL

AVERAGE ANNUAL RAINFALL

| MILLIMETERS | INCHES |
|---|---|
| Under 250 | Under 10 |
| 250–500 | 10–20 |
| 500–1,000 | 20–40 |
| 1,000–1,500 | 40–60 |
| 1,500–2,000 | 60–80 |
| Over 2,000 | Over 80 |

AVERAGE TEMPERATURE
(Isotherms, reduced to sea level, in degrees Fahrenheit)*

——— January
- - - - July

* Subtract approximately 3 degrees for every 1,000 feet of elevation.

Copyright by C. S. HAMMOND & Co., N.Y.

**Europe** Of the seven continents, Europe is next to the smallest. Only Australia is smaller. In spite of its size, it is the home of nearly one-fourth of the world's people.

### LAND FORMATION

On a map, Europe looks like a large PENINSULA of Asia. The two continents are so closely joined that geographers sometimes call them *Eurasia.* The boundary most used follows the Ural Mountains and River in Russia to the Caspian, and the crest of the Caucasus Mountains to the Black Sea.

On the south Europe is bounded by the Mediterranean Sea, on the west by the Atlantic Ocean, and on the north by the Arctic Ocean.

The continent of Europe covers 3,900,000 square miles. Europe boasts a staggering total of 25,000 miles of irregular coastline. This condition provides many excellent harbors.

1. *Mountains:* A relief map shows that there are numerous mountainous areas on the continent. What the map will not show is that Europe has seen the successive formation of four separate mountain chains and the destruction of three of them. The most recent is also breaking down.

Ancient remains of the *Huronian system,* the first chain, may still be seen in northwestern Scotland and far-northern Norway. A second chain, called the *Caledonian system,* partially remains in north Wales, southern Scotland and central Scandinavia, where altitudes of 4,000 to 6,000 feet may be observed. The third chain, the *Hercynian range,* lies across southwest England, southern Belgium and into central Germany. This arc may also be seen in central Spain and Portugal, in southern France and in some outcroppings as far as southern Russia.

The Alpine chain, which includes the Alps, Appenines, Dolomites, Carpathians, Balkans, Caucasus, and others, is the newest group of mountains. It has not worn down very much.

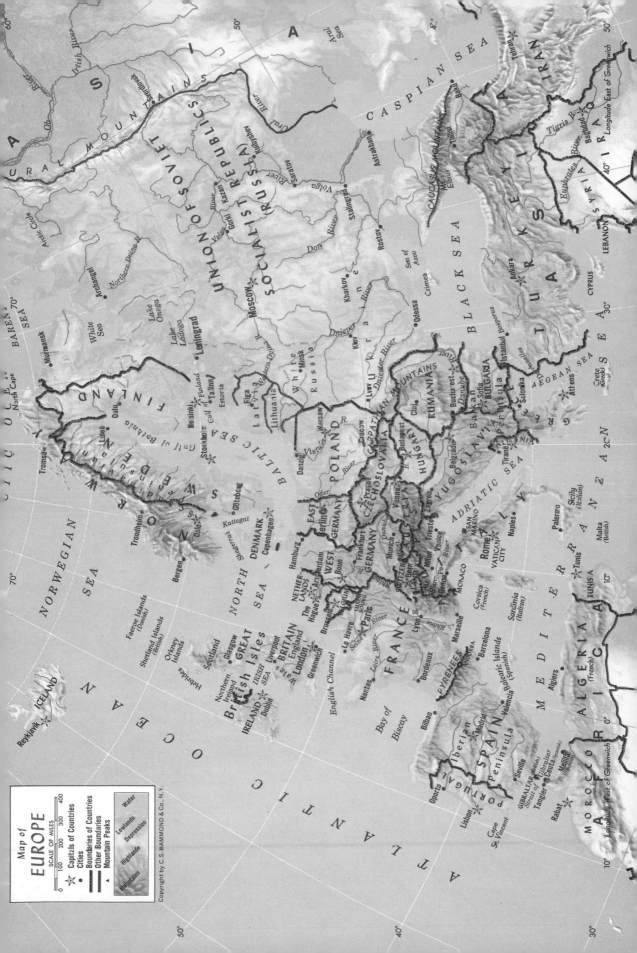

## Map of EUROPE

**SCALE OF MILES**

0  100  200  300  400

| | Capitals of Countries |
| :-: | :-- |
| ● | Cities |
| | Boundaries of Countries |
| | Other Boundaries |
| ▲ | Mountain Peaks |

Water
Lowlands
Highlands
Mountains
Depression

Copyright by C. S. Hammond & Co., N.Y.

2. *Plains:* One large section of the European land mass has resisted the mountains. This is the plains area extending across the Netherlands, lower Scandinavia, northern Germany, and the central plain of Russia. The area east of Scandinavia is sometimes called the *Baltic Shield* because of its resistance to the upward thrusting of the MOUNTAIN folds. Most of the area was covered by great ice sheets which appeared during the four GLACIAL AGES.

3. *Sea and land:* Throughout millions of years the continent has risen above and then sunk below the sea. During the time when the sea covered large areas, great deposits of chalk, coal and other MINERALS were laid down. The land is primarily the result of the formation and gradual breakdown of the earlier mountains.

The Black, Aegean, Adriatic, and Tyrrhenian seas were formed when the Alps upfolded. Elsewhere, large arms of the sea were completely isolated, and, as they slowly evaporated, huge deposits of salt remained. If European Russia is excluded, no place on the continent is more than 500 miles from either a sea or the ocean.

## CLIMATE

The climate of Europe falls into three main zones: (1) west and northwest Europe with mild temperatures and heavy rainfall; (2) central and eastern Europe, the region along the Alpine chain with more extreme temperatures and less rain; and (3) southern Europe with warm temperatures and winter seasonal rainfall. A minor region resembling the Arctic—northern Finland and Russia—has sub-polar climates with long, cold winters.

1. *West and northwest climate:* The British Isles, Portugal, western Spain, France, the Low Countries, Germany, and Scandinavia are in a region of mild temperatures, prevailing westerly winds mixed with strong cyclonic winds, and heavy rainfall. The annual rainfall averages from 170 inches in western Scotland, 80 inches at Bergen, Norway, to 40 inches in the interior of the mainland. The average seasonal temperature ranges about 20° F. between winter and summer.

2. *Central and eastern plains:* Land does not retain heat as long as water. Therefore, when the great plains of south Russia lose their heat in winter, they become severely cold. Since temperatures decrease with altitude, low temperatures prevail along the Alpine chain in a wedge that reaches as far west as the highlands of central Spain.

In Russia itself, seasonal temperatures vary from a January average of 20° F to a July average of above 70° F. In winter the cold, high pressure areas push the warmer layers of air out to the southwest and south. Under the summer sun the interior quickly heats, and the rising air creates low pressures, thus permitting the cooler, heavier air from the Atlantic to flow in along the same wedge-shaped route across the northern European plains. Rainfall is moderate throughout most of the central plains region.

3. *Mediterranean region:* Influenced by the great sea and the Sahara Desert, the winter low pressure lies over the Mediterranean and cold, moist air is drawn down from the north. With the coming of spring the high and low pressures become unstable. The winter rain, together with the melting Alpine snows, waters the region.

During the summer the Sahara Desert of AFRICA becomes quite hot. The high is then over Africa and low over the eastern Mediterranean. This causes a circulation of cool but dry summer breezes into the region, making it a favorite resort spot.

## RIVER AND DRAINAGE SYSTEMS

The formation of Europe is like a low mound, high in the center and low at the edges. For this reason, rivers of Europe flow from the center of the continent toward the seas in all directions.

The Seine, Rhine, Elbe, Oder, Vistula and Dvina rivers empty northward into the English Channel and North Sea. They drain the northern plains area. In the east, the Ural and Volga rivers of Russia flow southward. They empty into the Caspian Sea and drain the Russian plain. The Don River flows southward also, but into the Sea of Azov, an arm of the Black Sea.

Other important rivers also empty directly into the Black Sea. One of these rivers is the Dnieper. Another, the Dniester, rises in the Carpathian Mountains and flows eastward. Much of southeast Europe is drained by the Danube. It rises in the Black Forest of Germany, passes through the Alpine chain east of the Austrian Alps, and flows between the Balkan Mountains and Transylvanian Alps across the plains of Hungary, Rumania and Bulgaria into the Black Sea.

EUROPEAN WILD BOAR
4' long

JACKAL
2½' long

CHAMOIS
3½' long

IBEX
4' long

EUROPEAN
HARE
1½' long

EUROPEAN ANIMALS

EUROPEAN ELK
6' high
plus antlers

BADGER
2' long

AUROCHS or
EUROPEAN BISON
10' long

WOLF 4' long

REINDEER
4½' high
plus antlers

OTTER
3' long,
including
tail

MOUFLON
4' long

FOX 3½' long,
including 16"
tail

CRESTED PORCUPINE
3' long with quills

RED DEER
4' high plus
antlers

WEASEL
1' long

STORK
3' high

SQUIRREL
10" plus tail

RAT 8" plus tail

SHREW
4" plus tail

BROWN
BEAR
6' long

MEADOW
MOUSE
3½" long

LEMMING
6" long

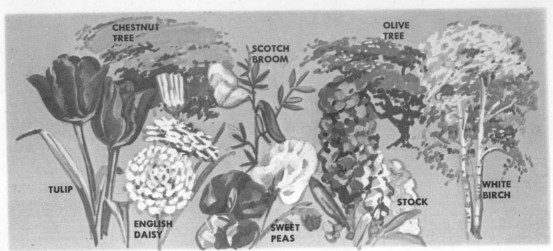

Some plants native to Europe

On the southern edge of Europe, the Po drops from the Alps to the north Italian plain and then into the Adriatic Sea. In France, the Rhone River emerges from Lake Geneva, and passing between the French Alps and the Cévennes range, empties into the Mediterranean Sea.

A distinctive feature of European topography is the great system of undrained marshlands. In Russia, the famous Pripet marshes have contributed greatly to the isolation of central Russia from western Europe. Most of these marshes are situated along the northern limits of the DECIDUOUS forests of the interior.

Similar marshes or bogs occur also in central Ireland and in Scotland. In the Arctic region extensive frozen marshes are found in northern Finland and the Kola Peninsula of northern Russia.

### PLANTS AND ANIMALS

The wildlife of Europe is largely the result of ancient migrations from Asia and north Africa. Plant growth is determined by climate and the conditions of the soil. The distribution of animal life is influenced by weather and by location of plants and other animals.

Some of the animals which long ago roamed the continent have disappeared. Others have been mixed with domestic animals and still exist as crossbreeds.

1. *Animals:* The chief European carnivores (the meat-eaters) are the brown bear, fox, wolf, otter, and badger. Wildcats are still present, though they are not as numerous as they used to be.

European deer are still found in some numbers. Reindeer of Lapland are well known. The chamois, a member of the ANTELOPE family which lives in the rocky highlands, is found only in Europe. Muskrats are found chiefly in the French highlands, and moles are common throughout the region.

Rabbits have generally spread northward over the entire continent. The brown rat has almost replaced the older black variety. Domestic animals include large numbers of famous breeds of horses. Cattle, swine, and numerous varieties of sheep are widespread. Sheep are especially numerous in the British Isles.

2. *Plants:* Zones of vegetation roughly correspond to the climatic zones. Most forms are thought to have migrated from the east and southeast in prehistoric times when the land rose from the oceans.

a. *Mediterranean:* Spain, Italy and the Balkan Peninsula are characterized by many

OLIVE trees. Plants in the region are of the tough, hairy leaf type well-suited to DROUGHT resistance. Woodlands contain evergreen oaks, Aleppo pines, and silver poplars. Smaller plants include oleander, myrtle, and laurel. Higher on the cool mountain slopes are extensive growths of BEECH trees. Tapering away from the forests are bush plants such as heather, arbutus, pistachio, and the mint plants such as sage. Various forms of grass, including alfalfa, thrive in the drier areas, as do the bulb plants such as onions. CITRUS FRUITS were introduced long ago from the lands of the Asiatic monsoon winds.

No description of Europe would be complete without some reference to the hundreds of varieties of grapes which grow throughout the region. Grapes are especially well-adapted to the soil and climate of Europe from the Mediterranean region as far north as the southern end of the Scandinavian peninsula.

b. *Oceanic zone:* Forests of this region are typically beech accompanied by OAK. The region extends up into the slopes of the Alpine chain where cool, moist climate provides ideal growth conditions for beech.

Fruits are abundant in much of the area. Plums, apples, cherries and other tree fruits are plentiful. Grapes abound in this region also. Humid, dark brown soil is very important here for sugar beets and potatoes, as well as other root crops. Bushy plants include gorse, bracken and varieties of heath along the coastal areas.

c. *Cold forests:* Outward from the region just described, beeches disappear and oaks continue to appear accompanied by ash trees. These give way in the colder regions to PINE and birch which are extensive in the north and also the upper Alpine slopes. In this latter region, larch is widespread and typical. The soil of the pine forests is not suited to agriculture. Hence, there is little point in clearing forests for that purpose.

The pine and dwarf birch extend toward the extreme northern fringes of Norway, Finland and Russia where the TUNDRA is frozen most of the year. Vegetation is sparse, quick-growing, and the flowering variety. Moss is widespread throughout the region.

d. *Central plains:* The eastern regions of the Russian steppes and great plains show a marked decrease in beech and oak, which disappear somewhere near the Ural Mountains. In southern Russia trees appear only along streams and consist mainly of willow, alder and poplar. Herbaceous plants include the tougher GRASSES, HEMP, and the quick-growing varieties with underground food supplies.

Wheat is widely grown, along with barley, rye, potatoes, and some sugar beets. On the northern fringe of the region are pine, birch, and willow, along with grasses, heather, mosses, and lichens.

## NATURAL RESOURCES

Europe is rich in many natural resources. Most important are coal, iron and aluminum.

Altogether Europe produces over 40% of the world's IRON. It is also the largest single source of BAUXITE from which aluminum is obtained. It has about 57% of the world's supply. The bulk of this ore is mined east of the Adriatic Sea, although France unearths over 20% of the total world output.

Other resources and their principal locations are COPPER in Yugoslavia, Spain, Germany and Scandinavia; MANGANESE in southeastern Europe; nickel from Norway; TUNGSTEN in Portugal; and chromite in the Balkans and Greece. Salt is mined in the eastern regions, and chalk in England and northwestern Europe. Northern Europe, led by Sweden, produces large quantities of timber and wood products. Fish are an important resource, and are found especially in the North and Norwegian seas.

COAL occurs abundantly in Great Britain, Germany, France, Poland and Belgium. As a whole, Europe supplies 46% of the world's coal. The story is different with the other fuels. NATURAL GAS is found in small amounts along the southern slopes of the Alps and in east and central Europe. But PETROLEUM is not plentiful with the exception of fields in France, Rumania and parts of Russia.

Production figures for natural resources of Europe generally do not include those of the Soviet Union. This is because no distinction is made between European and Asiatic Russia. If European Russia were included, increases in percentages of the world's output would appear in bauxite, manganese (Russia produces over 50% of the world total), chromite and coal.          W. J. K.

SEE ALSO: CONTINENT, CLIMATE, EARTH, NATURAL RESOURCES

## ✳ THINGS TO DO

**WHAT FACTORS AFFECT THE RATE OF EVAPORATION?**

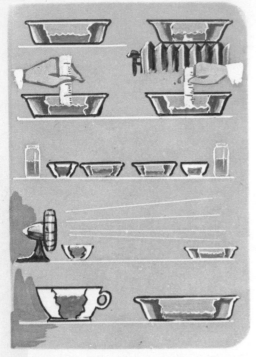

1   Pour a cup of water in a pan and set it to one side. Pour a cup of water in a second pan. Place this one over a source of heat for half an hour. Measure the amount of water left in both pans. What is the difference? The application of heat increases the rate of evaporation.

2   Pour a cup of liquid in each of three different sized containers—an olive jar, a bowl, and a cake pan. Let these stand for one day. Measure the amount of water left in each container. The greater the surface of liquid exposed, the greater the rate of evaporation.

3   Place an electric fan in front of a pan containing one cup of water. Put another pan of equal amount of water on the far side of the room. Turn on the fan for one hour. Measure the amount of liquid in the two vessels. Which has less? The fan blows away the moisture-laden air above the pan. Dry air comes in to take its place. The rate of evaporation is increased when wind is involved.

**Europium** (yoo-ROH-pee-um) Europium is an extremely rare element. It was discovered in 1901 by Eugene Demarcay. He named it after Europe. Europium is included in the RARE-EARTH series. It is a metal.

Europium (symbol Eu is element number 63. It has an atomic weight of 151.96 (152, O = 16). The metallic salts made from europium are light pink in color. The metal is often found in deposits of phosphate gravel and sand.                               J. R. S.
SEE ALSO: ATOM, ELEMENTS

**Eustachian tube** see Ear

**Evaporation** When a liquid, such as water, is placed in an open dish, after a period of time one notices the water has disappeared. Unless someone emptied the dish, the water changed into a GAS. This change from the liquid to the gaseous state is called *evaporation* or *vaporization*.

What is happening is that the particles that make up the water, MOLECULES, are moving in all directions with a variety of speeds. At any instant some molecules are moving fast enough to leave the surface and escape into the air. In this process all liquids absorb energy as they evaporate.          J. R. S.
SEE ALSO: PHYSICAL STATES AND CHANGES, WATER CYCLE

**Evergreen** Evergreen means "having green leaves all year." PINE, FIR, and SPRUCE trees are evergreens. Evergreen plants are the opposite of *deciduous* plants which shed their LEAVES in the fall.
SEE: PLANT; PLANTS, CLASSIFICATION OF

Evergreens lose their leaves a few at a time. Most of them have cones

JEAN BAPTISTE LAMARCK

CHARLES DARWIN

GREGOR MENDEL

ALFRED R. WALLACE

Many scientists contributed to the modern theory of evolution

**Evolution** Scientists believe that animals and plants of today have ancestors that lived millions of years ago. Instead of living in different parts of the world, these ancestors lived in the oceans. Of course, they looked very different from the plants and animals living in the ocean today. They looked more like the tiny cells which may be seen under a microscope.

A tree does not rise suddenly out of the ground. It grows slowly from a small seed in the earth. Each year it changes a little. After many years, it may have branches strong enough to hold a person. All living things change slowly. It took millions and millions of years for the ancestral forms in the ocean to become plants and animals living on land. There were millions of ancestors. Each ancestor changed a little.

Evolution really means *slow unfolding*. Scientists who study evolution study the ways in which plants and animals have changed. They do not always agree about the first ancestors.

### EARLY THEORIES

The theory of evolution is the result of the combined efforts of many people. The ancient scholars tell the story of creation and the establishment of the natural order in the Old Testament. It is told allegorically. For example, the "day" mentioned is only a symbol of a period of time—not 24 hours as time is measured today. Species were created that were capable of reproducing themselves and the natural order was thus established. The growth, selection, and evolution which followed could have taken millions of years.

But many superstitions—such as that horsehairs in rainwater turn into living worms—had arisen among primitive people, and scientists began to study and develop what was finally called the *Theory of Evolution*. An Italian doctor, Francesco Redi, proved that flies came, not from dead animals, but from eggs laid in the dead flesh by other flies.

# Evolution

Through the work of Redi, people began to understand that one living organism evolved, or came from, another living organism.

Several people began to wonder how individual differences arose among plants and animals. They wanted to know how new species developed. LAMARCK, a French scientist, decided that if a part of the body were used a great deal, it would grow larger with each generation. If a part were not used, it would grow smaller and disappear. Another scientist proved Lamarck to be wrong. By cutting off the tails of mice, he discovered that mice in each following generation were still always born with tails.

In the middle of the 19th century, two men, CHARLES DARWIN and Alfred Wallace, decided that the environment played an important part in causing differences to appear within the species. They pointed out that plants and animals depended not only upon one another for food but also upon a particular environment. As the environment changed, some plants and animals would die, and others, with characteristics more suitable to the new environment, would survive and reproduce.

A few years later, GREGOR MENDEL, an Austrian monk, decided that likenesses and differences between parent and offspring were passed on by means of factors, now called GENES. Genes are tiny units of a living cell, able to copy themselves. When there is only one parent, the new organism is similar to the parent. However, the copy or offspring always differs slightly from the original. When there are two parents, each parent passes on a set of genes to the offspring. If some genes *mutate,* or change, likenesses and differences appear in the offspring.

## NATURAL SELECTION

Plants and animals live in populations. They mate with members of the same species in the population and occasionally with members of the species in a neighboring population. For example, all cats in one town form a population of cats. Since they are members of the same species, they may mate with one another.

Since each member of the population possesses a set of genes, there are billions of genes available in one population. These genes are distributed randomly throughout the population. Any member of a species therefore has access to many combinations of genes. However, once a mate is selected,

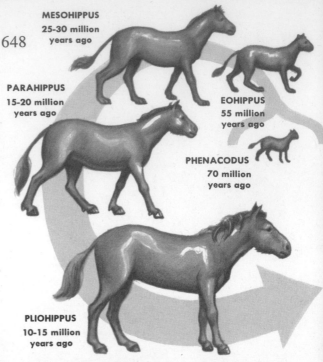

MESOHIPPUS
25-30 million
years ago

PARAHIPPUS
15-20 million
years ago

EOHIPPUS
55 million
years ago

PHENACODUS
70 million
years ago

PLIOHIPPUS
10-15 million
years ago

The evolution of the horse involved the change from a small animal with toes to a large one with hoofs. The changes were advantageous because of alterations in the land and food supply. The small wild horse of Russia looks most like the ancestral forms. Man has further helped the evolution of varieties of horses by breeding them for specific purposes

the genes available are limited to those possessed by the mate. If another mate were selected, another combination of genes would become available. Since some members of a species produce more offspring than others, their genes tend to become prevalent in the population. In general, those organisms that are best suited to live in their environment will produce more surviving offspring.

Every member of the population is free to select a mate of the same species and produce new combinations of genes. The action of the environment upon these new combinations is called *natural selection.* The organisms with gene combinations best adapted to the environment are most apt to survive and reproduce. This is what is meant by "survival of the fittest." In nature, many characteristics are selected again and again, while others are seldom selected. In the same way, certain cereals are always selected from the grocer's shelf, while others are rarely selected. Very soon, the cereals which are seldom selected disappear from the market. If cats with thin tails were seldom selected as mates by other members of the population, they would produce few offspring. The genes which produced the thin tails would become less prevalent.

PRZHEVALSKI'S HORSE — A few of these last wild horses still live in Asiatic Russia and Mongolia

HOW MAN HAS BRED HORSES FOR DIFFERENT USES — DRAFT HORSE — RACING HORSE — SADDLE HORSE

## ENVIRONMENTAL EFFECTS

The rate of evolution changes according to the environment. In the ocean, organisms have changed slowly. The salt and oxygen content and the temperature are more constant than on land. The green ALGAE and the horseshoe crab have not changed for millions of years. On land, where major geological changes occur, organisms have had to change more rapidly. The building and recession of mountains and glaciers are major changes. In cold climates, animals have developed heavy coverings of fur or feathers, while trees have produced seeds that withstand the winter.

When environmental changes occur, organisms must become adapted, migrate, or become extinct. But living organisms must wait for genetic changes. These changes often come too slowly to allow individuals to adapt to a new environment. Organisms which are less specialized are more likely to survive. If, for example, the plants of a grassland were killed, the animals which ate only plants must migrate or die. Those animals which ate different types of food would be more likely to survive.

There are geographical barriers, such as islands, mountains, oceans and deserts. Organisms are cut off from one another by soil and vegetation factors, temperature differences, and distance. If members of one species moved to a new territory to obtain more food, they might live too far apart to breed with members of the first population. If the climates of the two environments changed greatly, the members of the two populations might develop new structures. Due to differences in breeding season, chemical make-up, or individual rejection, members of the two populations might eventually be unable to mate. Thus the possible exchange of genes would end and a new species would be produced. The time required to produce a new species would probably be at least a million years, since the changes are gradual.

By artificial means, man has created new species and subspecies. Man has isolated and domesticated many wild species of plants and animals. The dog, horse and cow have been changed in body structure and hair development. Certain viruses, bacteria, and parasites which are pests or killers of plants and animals have been changed to new organisms by chemical means.

## THE PATTERN

As a young tree grows, it sends off new branches at the top. Smaller branches grow from these. The pattern of evolution is much like the form of a tree. One ancestor, like the first main branches, can give rise to many new descendants. The branches at the top represent the species living today. Often a branch, for some reason, dies. Other branches will fill the space or grow in its place. In evolution, as one organism becomes extinct, another organism, thousands or millions of years later, will fill its place.

Evolution is governed by natural selection and environmental change. Evolution can only change and remodel what is present in small, gradual steps.

### FOSSIL RECORDS

Fossils reveal much about evolution, since they are the preserved remains of organisms. They may be skeletons, shells, or carbon prints left upon rocks. When an animal has been trapped or buried in ice, sand, or swamp, the entire remains are sometimes found preserved.

FOSSILS are found in different earth layers. Since high land piles over low land, the deepest layers are the oldest. Deep layers reappear when soil erodes or land buckles and rises out of the ground during earthquakes. The age of rock may be estimated very closely. An entire fossil layer is likely to be of the same general age as the rock layer.

Although scientists think that life began about 2000 million years ago, fossil records cover only the past 500 million years. Thus, many theories are proposed to account for the origin of life and the development of the first plants and animals. Scientists compare present-day organisms both with one another and with fossils of different periods.

### THE COMMON ANCESTOR

Living creatures are composed of atoms and molecules. They are a direct product of the physical and chemical properties of the earth. As the gases of the earth cooled, billions of years ago, land, atmosphere, and oceans were formed. Living matter probably developed first in the OCEAN. Atoms combined to form molecules; molecules combined to form compounds. Eventually, ORGANIC COMPOUNDS, found only in living matter, were formed. As raw materials in the ocean became scarce, some molecules surrounded themselves with a thin shell of reserve food. They closely resembled the present-day virus, which is covered by a shell of protein. Finally, cells formed. They were probably surrounded by a thin membrane which kept the cell components separate from the ocean. They later developed a nucleus and were able to manufacture food, breathe, grow, and reproduce.

The great Irish elk developed larger and larger antlers that were an advantage in fighting. They became so large, however, that the weight of them was harmful and the species gradually died off

Chicago Natural History Museum

Early organisms began to find new ways of living. Some, like the virus, adopted a parasitic life, by living inside larger cells. Others started living on dead or decaying cells. Some cells developed molecules which allowed them to manufacture food by PHOTOSYNTHESIS, like green plants of today. Many cells developed openings or mouths which allowed them to consume other organisms, like animals of today.

Most scientists accept the theory that plants and animals descended from a common ancestor. The most likely type of ancestor is the *flagellate.* Although these organisms form a technical phylum classed as plants, they are still considered to be both plant and animal. Like plants, they have chlorophyll and carry on photosynthesis. Like animals, they propel themselves with a whip-like flagella and trap particles of food, which they ingest.

### THE FIRST PLANTS AND ANIMALS

The common ancestor must have produced at least three types of descendants. One type maintained the way of life of the parent and produced the modern flagellates. Another lost its plant characteristics and became an animal. The third line of descent lost its animal characteristics and became a plant.

The first plants were probably much like the one-celled green algae, which are successful in the ocean. Some algae developed different types of pigment, like those of the red and brown algae. This enabled them to live at greater depths where there is less light. Some became many-celled animals. For floating plants, a flat sheet of cells was an efficient type of structure.

The first animals were free to leave the surface of the ocean, since they no longer needed sunlight for the manufacture of food. They explored different types of locomotion, such as the *pseudopod* and *cilia.* Some, like the PROTOZOA, grew in size and became

Evolution of animals, like that of plants, probably began with a single-celled flagellate. Gradual development of two or three cell layers allowed more complex modifications

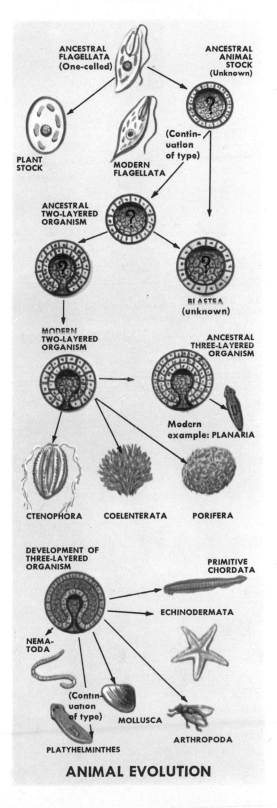

**ANIMAL EVOLUTION**

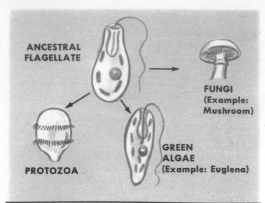

ANCESTRAL FLAGELLATE

FUNGI
(Example: Mushroom)

PROTOZOA

GREEN ALGAE
(Example: Euglena)

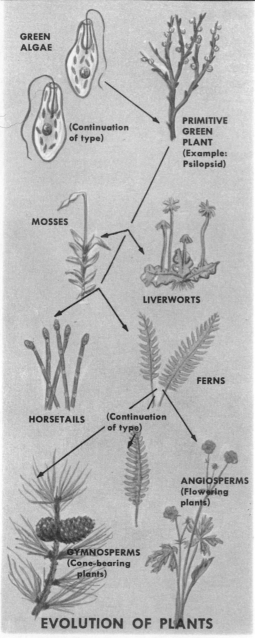

GREEN ALGAE

(Continuation of type)

PRIMITIVE GREEN PLANT
(Example: Psilopsid)

MOSSES

LIVERWORTS

HORSETAILS

(Continuation of type)

FERNS

ANGIOSPERMS
(Flowering plants)

GYMNOSPERMS
(Cone-bearing plants)

**EVOLUTION OF PLANTS**

successful one-celled animals. Others became multicellular. For moving animals, a hollow sphere of cells was a more efficient structure than a sheet of cells. The first multicellular animals were probably shaped like a hollow ball which consisted of one layer of cells.

The next step was the development of two and three body layers. Present-day animals like the sponges, coelenterates, and comb-jellies, are descendants of an ancestor which developed an inner layer of cells, called the *endoderm,* and an outer layer, called the *ectoderm.* The inner layer specialized in digestion, while the outer layer concentrated on protection. These two-layered animals, known as *diploblasts,* have remained in the ocean. The worms, mollusks, echinoderms, arthropods, and chordates are descended from an ancestor with three body layers, known as a *triploblast.* The third or middle layer, called the *mesoderm,* was an advantage. From the mesoderm arose systems for transportation for food and other body necessities. With this development the animal could increase in size, since food and gases could be circulated to the inner tissues.

## GEOLOGICAL PERIODS

During major geological changes, such as mountain and glacier building, plants and animals underwent great changes. Scientists have prepared a timetable to represent these geological events. The first period, known as the Azoic, meant "without life." Living organisms originated during the Pre-Cambrian period, which began 2000 million years ago. Although the fossil record is incomplete, it shows that one-celled organisms existed at this time.

Fossil records are more abundant for the three following periods. The PALEOZOIC ERA, which means "ancient life," began 500 million years ago. Every phylum of plants and animals in existence today was present at the beginning of this period. With the possible exception of bacteria, the land was free of organisms. At first, invertebrate animals and algae populated the ocean. Vertebrates appeared a little later. The agnatha or jawless fish, from which the present day LAMPREY EEL and hagfish de-

## EMBRYONIC PARALLELISM IN VERTEBRATES

STAGES OF
DEVELOPMENT
IN EACH:

EARLY

MIDDLE

LATER

MAN RABBIT CHICK FISH

**Similarities among embryonic forms of the chordates reveal, in part, their evolutionary relationship**

scended, were the first vertebrate fossils.

Plants were probably the first to invade land. The green algae produced tracheophytes, which developed roots, stems, leaves, and tissue, and reproduced by means of spores. Club mosses, horsetail, and ferns developed later, as separate descendants. FERNS grew to such enormous sizes that they formed great forests. One branch of the tracheophytes became the bryophytes, or MOSSES. Gymnosperms, the first seed plants, began to replace the ferns. The conifers (cone-bearing members) arose then.

In the ocean, new types of fish developed. Fish with jaws replaced the jawless fish. Cartilage fish like the sharks, skates, and rays appeared. There were three kinds of

bony fish—the ancestor of the fresh water fish, the lung fish, and the lobe-finned fish. As the sharks dominated the ocean, the bony fish probably moved to land and later became the ancestor of the amphibian.

As animals moved slowly to land, spiders, scorpions, snails and insects appeared. From amphibians, the first reptiles descended. These large, awkward animals were the first completely land vertebrates.

The MESOZOIC ERA, which means "middle life period," began about 200 million years ago. It is often called "the age of the reptiles," since these animals invaded the air and water and were dominant for 30 million years. Reptiles were ancestors of the birds, crocodiles, lizards, snakes, and turtles. The largest reptiles were the DINOSAURS, which walked on land, and the long-necked plesiosaur, which swam in the ocean. Therapsids, ancestors to the mammals, were descended from the reptiles. These animals walked on four feet, developed hair and became more mammal-like.

Among plants the angiosperms or flowering plants arose from the cone-bearing ancestors. These became the dominant land plants.

At the end of the Mesozoic Era, many of the reptiles became extinct. The CENOZOIC ERA, which means "new life period" and which has existed for the last 75 million years, has seen the development of the bird and mammals. These animals have filled the places left vacant by the reptiles.      E. P. L.

SEE ALSO: ANIMALS, CLASSIFICATION OF; EVOLUTION OF MAN; GEOLOGIC TIME TABLE; PALEONTOLOGY; PLANTS, CLASSIFICATION OF

**Evolution of man** All of the physical characteristics of man show that he is an animal. He has gone through many stages of growth and development as other animals have done. The animals most like man are the *anthropoid* (meaning "like man") apes. But even these apes do not have what man does—the abilities to think, reason, believe, and choose a course of action at will. These abilities are part of what is often called the "spirit" of man and they separate *human beings* from all other forms of life.

Modern science states that man as a physical creature, and as he is known today, has gone through the entire evolutionary process to make him a separate species of animal. The evolutionary theory of CHARLES DARWIN gives the best explanation of how man as we know him developed. By looking at the entire classification—or taxonomy—of modern man, the line of EVOLUTION behind him—millions and millions of years of it—can be seen.

Kingdom—Animal (all animals)
Phylum—Chordata (animals with a notochord)
Subphylum—Vertebrata (animals with a vertebral column replacing the notochord)
Class—Mammalia (animals that suckle their young and have hair)
Order—Primates (monkeys, apes and man)
Family—Hominidae (all forms of man)
Genus—Homo (man)
Species—sapiens (modern man)

The history of man is shown in FOSSILS. The first discovery of fossil man was made in the early 19th century. Since that time, the story of man's development has been pieced together. Often only single bones have been found. Sometimes these bones have been enough for men who study the development of man—physical anthropologists—to tell what part of the body they came from.

One thing that helps anthropologists in dating fossils is the geological layer of the earth's surface in which they were found. Over a period of almost one million years, four separate GLACIERS covered much of the earth. During each interglacial period—the time between glacial periods—there was a warm climate which helped evolution. The glaciers did not stop development because the animals could move south to where the ice did not reach. The fossils of man are usually dated according to the glacial period or interglacial period during which they lived.

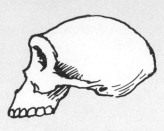

**ZINJANTHROPUS**

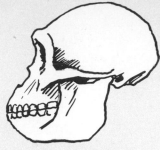

**AUSTRALOPITHECUS**

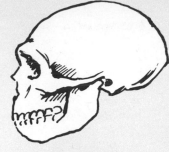

**PEKING MAN**

| TYPE OF MAN AND PLACE FOUND | PERIOD LIVED | BONES FOUND | BRAIN SIZE IN CUBIC CENTI-METERS |
|---|---|---|---|
| PREZINJANTHROPUS<br>Tanganyika, Africa | Preglacial (1,800,000 years ago) | Skull fragments, body bones of child | ?<br>(Gorilla is about 500cc.) |
| ZINJANTHROPUS<br>Tanganyika, Africa | Preglacial (1,750,000 years ago) | Skull | ? |
| AUSTRALOPITHECUS<br>(subfamily Australopithecinae)<br>Africa | 1st interglacial (500,000 years or more ago) | Skulls | 750cc. |
| CHELLEAN MAN<br>(named for tools)<br>Tanganyika, Africa | 2nd glacial (475,000 years ago) | Skull fragments | ? |
| PITHECANTHROPUS ERECTUS<br>(Java man)<br>Java | 2nd interglacial (450,000 years ago) | Skull, bone fragments, leg bone | 870cc. |
| SINANTHROPUS PEKINENSIS<br>(Peking man) (closely related to Java man)<br>Northern China | 2nd interglacial (150,000 years ago) | Almost complete skeletal material | 1075cc. |
| HOMO HEIDELBERGENSIS<br>(Heidelberg man)<br>Germany | 2nd interglacial 3rd glacial possibly earlier | Jaw bone | ? |
| HOMO SOLENSIS<br>(Solo man)<br>Java | 3rd interglacial 4th glacial (200-150,000 years ago) | Skull fragments | 1100cc. |
| HOMO RHODESIENSIS<br>(Rhodesian man)<br>Africa | 4th glacial (until about 50,000 years ago) | Skull, other bones are questionable | 1300cc. |
| HOMO NEANDERTHALENSIS<br>(Neanderthal man)<br>Asia, Africa, Europe | 3rd interglacial 4th glacial (disappeared about 25,000 years ago) | Many complete skeletons | up to 1600cc. |
| HOMO SAPIENS<br>(Cro-Magnon man)<br>France, Spain | 4th glacial (until about 12,000 years ago) | About 100 complete skeletons | up to 1800cc. |
| HOMO SAPIENS<br>(modern man)<br>All over | Since about 17,000 years ago | Complete skeletons | Average 1350-1400cc. |

NOTE: Because of the great age of the preglacial men as revealed by the potassium-argon dating process, the ages of the glacial men may be subject to change when further testing has been done.

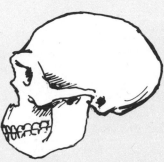

**NEANDERTHAL MAN**

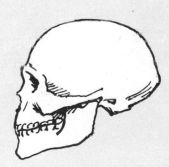

**CRO-MAGNON MAN**

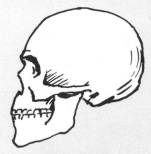

**MODERN MAN**

The Zinjanthropus "people" did not have real tools. In times when a ready supply of meat was not available, they probably cracked bones with rock to get at the marrow

Almost all human evolution happened during the Pleistocene. This is the period in the geologic time table of almost one million years just before the Recent Era which started 10,000 years ago and is still going on.

There were six major physical changes during the course of evolution from anthropoid to man. They are: (1) increased brain size—shown by increased capacity of the cranium; (2) development of a chin; (3) disappearance of heavy brow ridges above the eyes; (4) change to a vertical face; (5) shortening of the jaws; and (6) development of erect posture.

Each of the stages of man listed is considered a separate stage because the fossils show them to be different in the six major changes. There is evidence that among some of the fossils there are direct developmental relationships, but the lines of development are not always clear. In 1962, skull and jaw fragments of a creature now called *Kenyapithecus* were discovered. It had a jaw structure associated with speech though it probably did not speak. The fragments are 14 million years old according to the potassium-argon dating method. From this ape-man, there is a leap of more than 12 million years to *Zinjanthropus*.

In addition to the stages discussed, skull and bone fragments of many other man types shed a little more light on man's development. These include the Ternifine man, jaw fragments of Telanthropus and Kanam man —all of Africa; and the Swanscombe and Steinheim skulls and Combe-Capelle and Lautsch men of Europe.

*Prezinjanthropus:* In 1961, the skull and bones of a "child" killed by a blow on the head were found in Olduvai Gorge in Africa. Potassium-argon dating of the surrounding rock shows that the murder occurred more than 1,800,000 years ago. The fossils were found at a lower level than those of Zinjanthropus (below) and are about 50,000 years older. A hominid (not a true man) different from near men such as Australopithecus, the "Prezinj" creatures ate animals that could be caught by hand.

*Zinjanthropus:* The skull of Zinjanthropus, found in Olduvai Gorge in 1959, is the largest which has been linked to human evolution. Zinjanthropus is physically similar to Australopithecus (below) and was not a true man. He lived about 1,750,000 years ago. His culture was a true Stone Age culture, with tools made in a regular, set pattern. He was not a very skillful hunter and was able to kill only the young of large animals.

*Australopithecus:* This southern ape (*Australo* = southern, *pithecus* = ape) was not human. It lived during the first interglacial and second glacial periods in southern Africa. The Australopithecus has been placed by anthropologists in a sub-family of the "true" man (euhominid) because it was still so much like an ape. It is related to man because of its man-like teeth (dentition) and its upright walk. Only skulls of the southern ape have been found. They were discovered in 1924. This ape belonged to the type Australopithecine.

*Pithecanthropus erectus* (Java man): The steps from Australopithecus to "true" man is not clear. This Java man is the first that can be called definitely human. The skeleton, skull and teeth found were all those of humans. The brain case is larger than that of the apes. He stood erect and killed animals for food. He also knew the use of fire. His culture was probably similar to that of the Peking man, although no real artifacts —man-made articles—have been found that can be traced to him. The Java man may be the direct ancestor of the Australian aborigines of today.

*Sinanthropus pekinensis* (Peking man): Almost complete skeletons from several individuals of Peking man have been found, mostly in China. They lived during the early Pleistocene. The adult was about five feet tall. He had no chin and still had heavy brow ridges of the ape. His mouth and teeth were smaller than Java man's. Java and Peking men were closely related in many ways. They are often classed together as types of species *Homo erectus*.

The Peking man made sharp tools from flint—a kind of quartz. Hammers, scrapers and simple instruments of bone have also been found. He cooked with fire and ate meat, bone marrow, plants and berries. It is fairly certain that he had some kind of simple language. The Peking man may be the ancestor of the mongoloid races.

*Chellean man:* Although the tools of this true man were found as long as 100 years ago, the first skull was found in Olduvai Gorge in 1960. Chellean man lived during the second glacial age. He was a huge and powerful hunter, bringing down huge animals with a weapon made of heavy weights connected by thongs, much like the bolas used by the gauchos in South America today. He liked color, for lumps of red ocher, which was not available near by and had to be brought from a considerable distance, have been found at his campsites.

The Java men were probably the first animals to cook their meat with fire. The climate of Java was probably colder than it is today

E. GRAF

**Chellean men used the bola—stones on the end of a leather thong—as a weapon. Accurate throwing made the thongs wrap themselves around the legs of animals**

*Homo heidelbergensis* (Heidelberg man): The fossils of the Heidelberg man are the oldest human fossils known. They were probably a separate line of development from Peking and Java men. Heidelberg man —usually the first to be designated as genus *Homo*—lived during the first and second interglacial periods. Thus, though he is from about the same time as the other men, he was further developed toward modern men. Geological charts show him to be three-fourths of a million years old. The jaw that was found in Germany was ape-like, but the teeth in it were human.

The remains were found with fossil elephants, bears, deer, cats, bison, beavers and two kinds of horses. The animals were mostly like the ones today. The climate was very warm, so Heidelberg man probably had an easy life. He had only the simplest tools and a simple language. Anthropologists disagree on the age of *Homo heidelbergensis*. Some say that he should be placed earlier in the list.

*Homo solensis* (Solo man): Eleven skulls and some leg fragments of this man were found in the Solo River of Java. He lived during the third interglacial or fourth glacial period. The skull of the Solo man is much longer and higher than that of the Peking or Java man. But the brain size was about the same, because the skull was thick. No face bones are available so anthropologists are unable to say what he looked like. His stone tools were very primitive, but the bone tools were beautifully and artfully made. Solo man lived at the same time as the Neanderthal and Rhodesian men but was not as well developed.

*Homo rhodesiensis* (Rhodesian man): The skull of the Rhodesian man was found in South Africa in 1921. Some other bones were found, but there is some question whether they belong to the skull. If they do, he was about five feet ten inches tall and weighed about 210 pounds. He was very powerful. He walked erect and looked somewhat like the Peking man. Rhodesian man may be an ancestor of the negroid race.

*Homo neanderthalensis* (Neanderthal man): This man lived around the Mediterranean Sea. The first of the many skeletons found was discovered in the Neanderthal valley of Germany. He lived during the third interglacial period and became extinct toward the middle of the fourth glacial period. No one knows why.

The Neanderthals had a fairly complex culture including magic, language, and regular hunting for food. Families lived in caves or in shacks they built. They did no farming. Their tools were of flint and bone. They were smart enough to make traps for the animals that lived near—hyenas, saber-toothed tigers, bears and leopards. They used the animal skins for clothing. Just before they disappeared abruptly, they started burying tools with the dead.

The Neanderthal man still had heavy brow ridges and little chin. He walked slightly stooped. The brain sizes were larger than modern man's.

*Cro-Magnon man* (the first *Homo sapiens*): This man probably lived late in the Pleistocene during the fourth glacial period, although some Cro-Magnon bones have recently been found in earlier deposits. The Cro-Magnon man is known mainly for the beautiful art work he left behind on cave walls all over Europe. He also had highly polished and decoratively-carved tools.

The first skeleton found was painted red and buried with jewelry, shells and other implements. Their complex religion may have dictated this so the dead could use the tools in an afterlife. Cro-Magnon man lived in caves. The climate was probably cold and unpleasant because this was a glacial era. Cro-Magnon man was a skillful hunter, killing MAMMOTHS, reindeer, musk oxen, horses, bears and lions. He resembled modern man but had a somewhat larger skull and more powerful body.

*Modern man* (also *Homo sapiens*): Man, as he is known today, is largely the same as Cro-Magnon with some physical refinements. There are three main races which make up *Homo sapiens*. Anthropologists do not know how they first became differentiated. The differences are not in color or nationality, but in such physical characteristics as head shape, bodily proportions, type of hair, ratio between head length and width (called *cephalic index*) and nose shape. The three main races are Negroid, Caucasoid, and Mongoloid.

Modern man has used his brain to develop a complex culture. Evolution has not stopped, and there are, in general, two directions which further development of man can take. He can be lost as earlier men were lost, perhaps destroying himself, or further refinement of his brain may lead him to an even greater dominance and utilization of the earth and its resources.     J. F. B.

SEE ALSO: ANIMALS, CLASSIFICATION OF; GLACIAL AGES; GEOLOGIC TIME TABLE; HUMAN BEING; LAMARCK, JEAN; PALEONTOLOGY; TAXONOMY

**Ewe** see Sheep

Neanderthal men wore animal skins as clothes. They probably dried the skins by pegging them out in the sun and used scrapers of flint for cleaning them

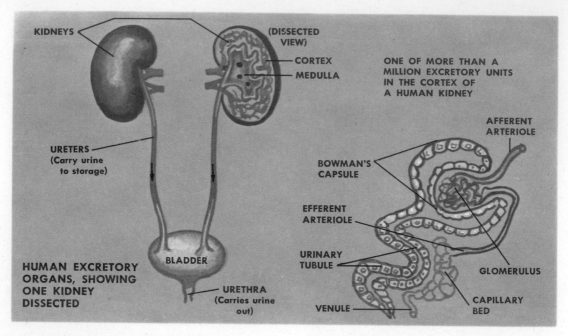

KIDNEYS

(DISSECTED VIEW)

CORTEX
MEDULLA

ONE OF MORE THAN A MILLION EXCRETORY UNITS IN THE CORTEX OF A HUMAN KIDNEY

AFFERENT ARTERIOLE

URETERS (Carry urine to storage)

BOWMAN'S CAPSULE

EFFERENT ARTERIOLE

URINARY TUBULE

BLADDER

GLOMERULUS

HUMAN EXCRETORY ORGANS, SHOWING ONE KIDNEY DISSECTED

URETHRA (Carries urine out)

VENULE

CAPILLARY BED

*The kidneys with their many tubules are vital parts of the human excretory system*

**Excretory system** (ECKS-kruh-tory) All animals must have a way to pass waste products out of their bodies. This is usually taken care of by an excretory system. In simple animals that have only one unit or cell for a body, waste is passed through the cell surfaces and also through the contractions of an organ-like bubble containing water and waste.

An animal like a sponge, even though it has a body made of many cells, is built upon such a simple plan that waste may still be passed through the cell surfaces.

The body plan of an EARTHWORM is not as simple, because different kinds of body cells are grouped together to do certain kinds of work for the body. These groups of cells working together may be called *organs*. Some of these organs digest food, circulate blood, and eliminate waste. Since the body of an earthworm is divided into a series of

sections or segments, each segment has two organs to take care of eliminating waste. These are called the *nephridia*. Each one consists of a coiled tube. One end of the tube looks like a very small funnel lined with small moving hairs named *cilia*. The other end of the tube opens to the outside of the body. The current made by the moving cilia draws waste particles from the body fluid into the tube which passes them out of the body.

In the human excretory system there are two bean-shaped KIDNEYS, one on each side of the body. Each is connected to the bladder by a canal or duct, the *ureter*. The bladder, a sac-like organ, opens to the outside of the body through another duct, the *urethra*. The waste materials in the body are collected by the blood. As the blood flows through the kidneys, most of the waste materials and extra water are taken out. The mixture of water and waste taken from the blood by the kidneys is called URINE. It passes down the ureters to the bladder and is stored there. When the bladder becomes full, it is emptied through the urethra by passing the urine out of the body.

The basic unit of the kidney is called the *renal tubule,* and the kidney is made up of many of these units. The tubule begins with a tuft of capillaries, the *glomerulus,* surrounded by a capsule (*Bowman's capsule*). The glomerulus connects with a coiled looped tube (*convoluted tubule*) which in turn connects with a main collecting tubule. These tubules open into a part of the kidney called the *renal pelvis,* which is actually the upper part of the ureter.

The ureter, about 11–14 inches long, narrows as it leaves the kidney and becomes about half as small in diameter before it enters the bladder. The wall of the ureter has three coats or layers. The inner layer is of EPITHELIAL TISSUE with many mucous secreting cells. The middle layer is muscular, some of the muscles running lengthwise and some in a circular direction around the tube. The outer coat is fibrous and contains nerves and blood vessels.

The *bladder* is a hollow, muscular, thin-walled organ which is oval in shape when full of urine. When completely empty its walls are in contact with each other. The capacity of the adult bladder varies from 6–24 ounces of fluid. The layers making up the wall of the bladder are similar to those in the ureter. However, the muscle layer is thicker and beneath the epithelium is a submucosa tissue layer. This layer allows the freedom of movement between the epithelial and muscular layers necessary to an organ that changes size and shape. The *urethra* carries urine from the bladder to the outside.                    J. C. K.

**Exocrine glands** see Endocrine glands

**Exoskeleton** An exoskeleton is a hard cover on the outside of an animal. It protects the soft inner parts of the body. The shells of clams, lobsters and oysters are exoskeletons. The opposite of an exoskeleton is an ENDOSKELE-TON (internal skeleton).

SEE: ANIMALS, CLASSIFICATION OF; CHITIN; CRAYFISH

**Exothermic** Exothermic refers to a chemical change in which HEAT is given off. Exothermic is the opposite of ENDOTHERMIC.

## ✳ THINGS TO DO

### WILL GASES EXPAND?

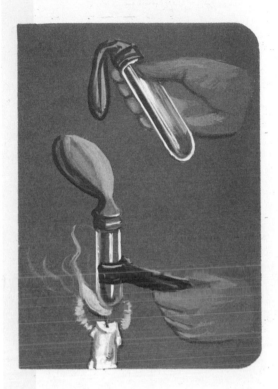

1 **Pull the mouth of a small balloon over the opening of an empty (though contains air) test tube. Using tweezers hold the test tube over a candle flame.**

2 **What happens to the balloon?**

3 **Heat makes the molecules of air move faster and farther from each other. Air in the tube expands. It escapes into the balloon causing it to fill up.**

**Expansion** Expansion is the increase in length, area or volume of a substance when it is heated. Expansion occurs in solids, liquids and gases. Gases expand more than liquids when the rise in temperature is the same, and liquids expand more than solids.

Substances vary in the amount of expansion for each degree rise in temperature. Among the metals, aluminum expands more than 2½ times as much as platinum with equal heat change. The expansion of mate-

✳ **THINGS TO DO**

**WILL LIQUIDS EXPAND?**

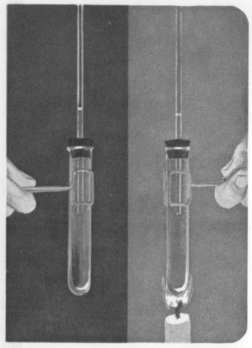

Materials: test tube, one-holed rubber stopper or drill a hole in a cork, glass tube several inches long, candle, colored water.

1   Fill the test tube with colored water. Insert the stopper in which the glass tube has been placed.
2   With tweezers or tongs, hold the test tube over the candle flame.
3   Does the water rise in the tube? Liquids expand when heated. Does this explain the action of mercury in a thermometer?

rials must be considered in all construction work. The tar between sections of highway, for example, allows the concrete to expand in winter.

Water is an exception to the rule that most substances expand when heated. When water is heated from 0°C. to 4°C., it contracts and becomes more dense. Above 4°C., water expands. This accounts for ponds freezing on the top instead of the bottom, allowing fish to survive under the ice.                                    J. H. D.

SEE ALSO: BOYLE'S LAW, GAS, KINETIC THEORY, MOLECULAR THEORY

✳ **THINGS TO DO**

**WILL SOLIDS EXPAND?**

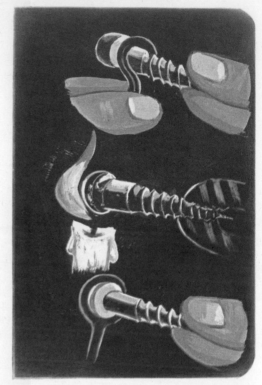

1   A commercial ball and ring may be used for this experiment. A home-made device may be assembled with a hook-eye and screw. The hook-eye can be adjusted so the screw just slips through the eye of the hook.
2   With tongs, hold the screw over the flame of a candle for a few minutes.
3   Now try to insert it through the opening in the hook-eye.
4   What happened to it? Metal expands when heated.

**Experiment** An experiment is a test made to confirm something which is known or to find out something not yet known. Taking the temperature of boiling water is an experiment confirming something known—the temperature at which water boils. Examining the effects of a new chemical compound on rats is an experiment to discover what is not yet known.

SEE: SCIENTIFIC METHOD

**Expiration** Expiration, or exhalation, is the breathing out of air from the LUNGS. It is opposed to *inspiration*, or inhalation, the breathing in of air.
SEE: RESPIRATORY SYSTEM, TRANSPIRATION

**Explosives** Any substance which changes from a small volume to a large volume in a very short period of time and causes violent reactions is called an *explosive*. During the time it is changing from a small to a large volume, a large amount of ENERGY is released into the surrounding gases and causes rapid expansion, or the explosion.

Although explosives are generally considered as part of warfare, they have many peaceful uses. The blasts can be controlled and used to tunnel roads through mountains, dig canals, clear land, blast out rocks, and open mines.

A good explosive must meet several requirements. It must not explode under ordinary conditions. It must be easy to manufacture and safe to ship to other places. It must also produce the desired results. For example, GUNPOWDER must propel a projectile without shattering the gun barrel or injuring the person firing the gun. If an explosive is to shatter and lift stumps or rocks, it must do only this.

Most explosives contain the elements carbon, hydrogen, oxygen, and nitrogen, as well as other elements that help to determine the type of explosion which will result. Explosives may be divided into two or sometimes three groups. The cause of the explosion or the way in which the energy is released is the factor that decides in which group an explosive belongs. Propellants or low explosives, primary explosives or initiators, and high explosives are the three groups.

*Propellants* burn instead of actually exploding. They are often called *low explosives* as they are slower and less powerful than other explosives. Black powder or common gunpowder is a propellant. It is the oldest explosive and is used in firecrackers. It was used before there were guns. Smokeless powder, used in shotgun shells, is another propellant.

PROPELLANTS DO NOT TURN TO GAS ALL AT ONCE BECAUSE THEY BURN IN A SERIES OF SMALL EXPLOSIONS

HIGH EXPLOSIVES TURN TO HOT, EXPANDING GASES IN AN INSTANT

*Primary explosives* or *initiators* do not burn but explode from a spark, flame, or sudden jar or blow. They are used to *detonate* or set off high and more powerful explosives. They produce violent explosions with noise and shock waves. Mercury fulminate and lead azide are examples of primary explosives.

*High explosives* change from solids or liquids to gases very quickly. They are made to explode by the shock of another explosion. Guncotton, cotton treated with sulfuric and nitric acids, is a high explosive that explodes violently when compressed into a small space. DYNAMITE, nitroglycerine, TNT (trinitrotoluene), and RDX (cyclonite) are other common high explosives.

J. D. B.

SEE ALSO: BOMBS, WEAPONS

**Extension** see Muscle system

**Extrasensory perception** Extrasensory means *outside* the senses. Extrasensory perception (called *ESP*) is being aware of, or knowing about outside events without any sensory stimulation coming from the events themselves. For example, if a child can describe a new dress her teacher is going to wear to school the next day, without having been told about the dress or ever having seen it, that child's knowledge may come from ESP. The outside event is the dress her teacher is going to wear. There is no sensory stimulation because her knowledge did not come from remembering what she heard (auditory stimulation) or saw (visual stimulation).

In a guessing game often played by children, one child says, "I see something. What do I see?" The rest of the children in the group try to guess what object the first child sees. The children who are guessing may ask questions that can be answered by yes or no. One child in the group might make a lucky guess and name the object without having asked any questions. If this same child continues guessing the objects correctly more than half of the time his knowledge of the correct object may be more than just luck. The child may have a kind of ESP called *mental telepathy*.

In mental telepathy, one person knows something because of a sensory stimulus and another person does not. The child who says "I see something" actually sees the object and is responding to a visual stimulus received from the object. The child who guesses is not responding to this stimulus.

If the child guessing knows, more than half the time, what object the child who says "I see something" is going to select before he chooses it, the guesser is said to be showing another kind of ESP, *precognition*.

Many scientists believe that there is not enough evidence to prove the existence of ESP and that the methods used in obtaining the evidence are not accurate.     J. C. K.

**Extremities** The extremities of an animal are the appendages. They may be more specifically defined as the extreme end of the appendages, such as the hands of the arm, the feet of the legs, or the pincers of a CRAYFISH.
SEE: SKELETON

**Eye** Sight is one of the most important senses of human beings, and the eye is the organ of sight. It is globular in shape. Humans have two eyes. They are located in two bony cavities in the front part of the skull which, together with the eyelids, protect them. The upper lids can close to cover and moisten the exposed portion of the eyes. This protects them from bright light and from foreign substances.

The inner portion of the eyelids are covered with a very thin membrane which begins at the top of the lid and continues over the exposed surface of the eyeball, extending itself as lining for the lower eyelid. This membrane, the *conjunctiva,* contains many nerves and serves as a protective covering. Whenever foreign substances, such as dust particles, enter the eye the conjunctiva becomes irritated and causes pain which continues until the substance is removed. The eyelashes also help to keep injurious particles from entering the eye.

The eyeball consists of three coats of tissues. Most of the outer coat is made up of tough FIBROUS TISSUE and is called the *sclerotic coat*. It is the white portion of the eye which can be seen. At the center of the eye, the sclerotic coat becomes transparent and is known as the *cornea*.

Behind the sclerotic coat is the *choroid coat,* composed of a vascular tissue which nourishes the eye. The choroid coat extends from behind the eyeball and joins with tissues called the *ciliary body*. It is chiefly composed of two parts, the ciliary muscle and ciliary processes. There are from 60 to 80 ciliary processes. They consist essentially of blood vessels and secrete nutrient fluids which nourish the cornea, the lens and part of the vitreous humor. At the front of the eyeball, in the center, the choroid coat becomes modified (changed) to form the *iris,* a ring of pigmented muscles which give the eye color. The iris has an opening in the center known as the *pupil*.

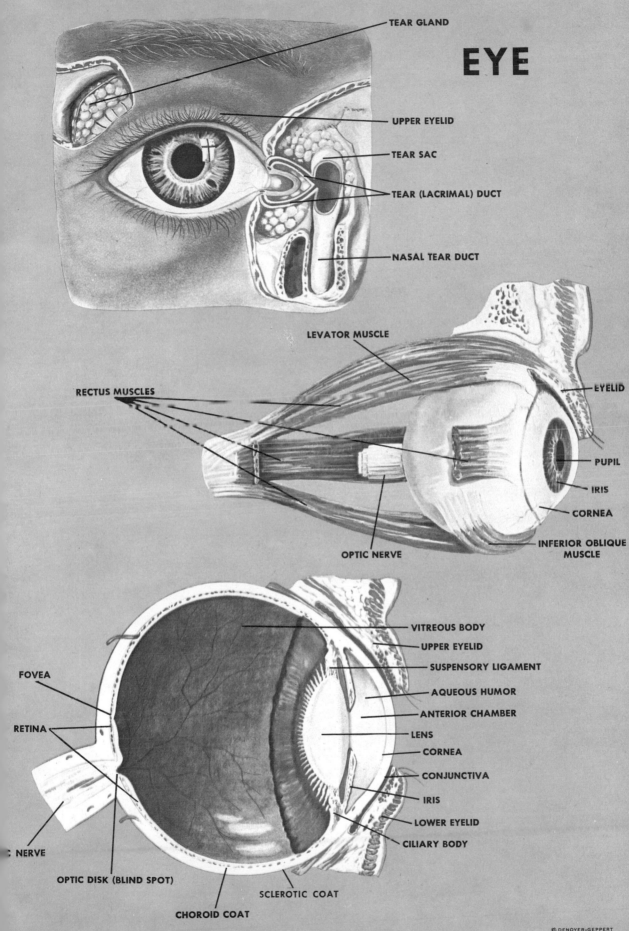

# EYE

TEAR GLAND

UPPER EYELID

TEAR SAC

TEAR (LACRIMAL) DUCT

NASAL TEAR DUCT

LEVATOR MUSCLE

RECTUS MUSCLES

EYELID

PUPIL

IRIS

CORNEA

INFERIOR OBLIQUE MUSCLE

OPTIC NERVE

VITREOUS BODY

UPPER EYELID

SUSPENSORY LIGAMENT

AQUEOUS HUMOR

ANTERIOR CHAMBER

LENS

CORNEA

CONJUNCTIVA

IRIS

LOWER EYELID

CILIARY BODY

FOVEA

RETINA

C NERVE

OPTIC DISK (BLIND SPOT)

SCLEROTIC COAT

CHOROID COAT

© DENOYER-GEPPERT

## ✳ THINGS TO DO

### WHERE IS THE BLIND SPOT IN YOUR EYE?

1 Put two small (⅛ inch) dark squares on a sheet of light-colored paper.

2 Hold this sheet at arm's length in front of your face. Close the right eye and stare at the right square. Bring the paper slowly toward your eyes.

3 At what point did the left square disappear? Did it reappear when the paper was moved closer?

4 The point on the retina where the optic nerve enters is called the blind spot since it lacks nerve endings. When the light rays from an object hit this spot, the impulse is not received.

### ARE YOU RIGHT-EYED OR LEFT-EYED?

1 Hold your finger out in front of you. Line it up with some object across the room.

2 Close your left eye. Now open your left eye and close your right.

At which time did it appear that your finger jumped to the side? If the finger stays lined up with the object when your right eye is open, you are right-eyed.

### HOW DOES THE IRIS IN YOUR EYES WORK?

1 Look into a mirror. Note the size of the pupils. They are the black circles —the opening in the iris, the colored part of your eyes. They are now adjusted to lamp or daylight.

2 Now have someone shine a flashlight into your face. Watch the size of the pupils.

3 Did the iris close down the opening? How does this help you see better?

The innermost coat of the eye is called the *retina*. It is the nerve tissue of the eye and is considered an expansion of the optic nerve. The point at which the optic nerve penetrates the eyeball is called the *blind spot*. Below and slightly to the side of the optic disc is a yellow circular area called the *macula*. There is a depression, the *fovea centralis,* in the center of this area. This is the point of most distinct vision. Behind the iris lies the *lens*—a semi-solid transparent body enclosed in a capsule. The lens is connected with the ciliary body by ligaments.

There is a space between the cornea and the lens which is filled with a watery liquid called *aqueous humor*. This liquid is secreted by the ciliary processes.

Behind the lens is a larger cavity filled with a gelatin-like material called *vitreous humor*. This material is enclosed in a capsule called the *hyaloid membrane*.

Above the eyeball is found the *lacrimal gland* or tear gland. It produces a fluid which keeps the eyeball moist.

To see images clearly, rays of light entering the eye must pass through the cornea, aqueous humor, and through the pupil, an opening which changes in size according to the amount of light entering it. The iris controls the changing of the pupil's size. The light rays continue on through the lens, which thickens or flattens out to allow the light rays to focus properly on the retina. The ciliary muscles act to change the shape of the lens. This power of adjustment of the lens is called *accommodation*. After passing through the lens, the light rays traverse the vitreous humor and finally focus on the retina in the normal eye. The retina is that sensitive inner coat of the eyeball which records the images. The impulse is sent along the optic nerve to the thalamus and the midbrain.

Fibers from the optic nerve make connections with cells in the retina. Because of their shapes, these cells are called *rods and cones*.

In the human eye, in the cell layer of the retina opposite the lens, there are about 125 million rods and seven million cones. These cells are the visual receptors for sight. The cones are concerned with vision of bright, colored light and the rods with dim, colorless vision. The rods and cones contain a photosensitive pigment known as *visual purple* appearing along their outer segments only.

The most accepted theories of vision explain sight as chemical changes in these photo-sensitive pigments that stimulate the rods and cones to transmit visual impulses along the optic nerves.

Movements of the eye are controlled by several muscles which make it possible to move the eye from side to side, up and down, and to rotate it slightly.     G. A. D.

SEE ALSO: ASTIGMATISM; CATARACT; COLOR BLINDNESS; EYE, BINOCULAR; EYE, COMPOUND; EYE, SIMPLE; FARSIGHTEDNESS; LENS, MAN-MADE; NEARSIGHTEDNESS; NERVOUS SYSTEM; OPTICAL INSTRUMENTS; OPTOMETRY

## ✳ THINGS TO DO

### WHAT IS THE FUNCTION OF THE RODS AND CONES IN THE EYES?

1  Look straight ahead.
2  Have someone hold a sheet of colored paper at arm's length out to the side of your body. Can you see what color the paper is?
3  Slowly swing the arm forward until the paper is directly in front of the eyes. Can the color be recognized now?
4  The nerve endings called rods are located in the outer rim of the retina. They distinguish light and dark. The nerve endings situated in the center of the retina are the cones which are stimulated by color.

**Eye, binocular** Two eyes working together can see better than one eye working alone. In binocular vision (with two eyes) each eye registers a slightly different picture. Then the brain interprets, and combines them to give the single picture "seen." Such vision helps tell how far away things are. One EYE working alone is called *monocular* vision.

Vision with one eye is flat and dull (left); binocular vision gives color and depth (right)

**Eye, simple** The simple eye may be merely a spot composed of cells that are sensitive to LIGHT. It is unable to see definite objects. It senses only the light and the direction from which the light comes. WORMS and STARFISH are some animals with this kind of eye. A simple eye is the "ancestor" of the complex eye of man.

The cells sensitive to light may be surrounded by dark pigmented cells and may have a transparent lens-like covering which focuses the light. The simple eyes (*ocelli*) of arthropods are of this type. Arthropods may have compound eyes also.

The squid and octopus have a more efficient simple eye. It is rounded and deeper, possibly forming an image, though with a small field of view. It is a "camera eye" like that of man.                    E. M. S.

SEE ALSO: ARTHROPODA; EYE

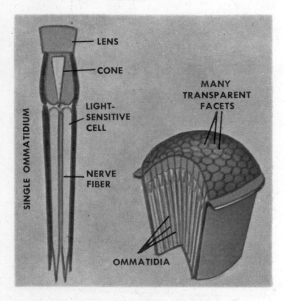

SINGLE OMMATIDIUM

LENS

CONE

MANY TRANSPARENT FACETS

LIGHT-SENSITIVE CELL

NERVE FIBER

OMMATIDIA

Compound eye of an insect showing facets

**Eye, compound** The compound eye (or *ommateum*) is made of many small eyes called *ommatidia* packed closely together. The common housefly has compound eyes.

The compound eye must be directed toward the light. When the light is directly over an ommatidium, the light ray passes through the transparent covering (*facet*) to the light-sensitive tissue at the opposite end. The light reaches and is directly over first one ommatidium then another, thus recording motion.

The sum of the resulting images sent to the brain appears either as a mosaic of dark and light or differently colored blocks. This visual process is especially well adapted for recording motion since any change in the position of an object affects the entire pattern of ommatidia.                    E. M. S.

Advanced simple eye of a spider

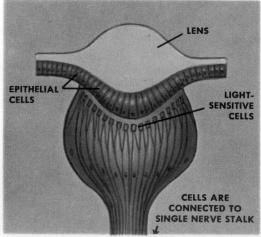

LENS

EPITHELIAL CELLS

LIGHT-SENSITIVE CELLS

CELLS ARE CONNECTED TO SINGLE NERVE STALK

Jean Fabré

**Fabré, Jean** (FAH-bray, ZHAIIN) (1823–1915) Jean Fabré was a French naturalist who devoted his entire life to the study of insects. The books he wrote are almost as readable as fairy tales.

Born in Saint-Léons in Aveyron, southern France, Fabré spent all of his life in that region. His poverty made it impossible for him to travel, so he studied the insects native to that small area. He was particularly interested in the spider, fly, bee, grasshopper, and wasp. Most of his knowledge was gained by direct observation.

Despite his poverty, Fabré managed to get a university degree, and became a teacher in the secondary school at Avignon. His textbooks in elementary science were used by thousands of children in France, but he was almost unknown outside of France. It was not until he was nearly eighty years old that people became aware of his greatness and rescued him from poverty. His most important work, *Souvenirs Entomologiques,* was recognized and honored by the French Academy, and the French government gave him a pension the last five years of his life.

           D. H. J.

**Factor** see Algebra, Mathematics

**Fahrenheit** Fahrenheit was the name of a German scientist. His name is given to a scale used to measure temperature. In English-speaking countries, weather, body temperatures, and oven heat are commonly measured on the Fahrenheit scale.

A mercury thermometer is marked at 32 degrees Fahrenheit (32°F) when the expanding mercury at that height is as cool as melting ice. The height is marked at 212 degrees when the mercury is as warm as boiling water. The space between is marked into 180 equal intervals, each a degree.

           H. W. M.

SEE ALSO: CALORIE, THERMOMETER

**Faint** A faint is a sudden loss of consciousness due to a lack of oxygen and glucose in the brain. The most common cause is a fall in BLOOD PRESSURE due to a severe emotional reaction such as fear.

**Fairy ring** see Mushroom

**Falcon** (FAWL-kuhn) Falcon is the name given to several kinds of long-winged birds. They are called BIRDS OF PREY because they swoop down from the sky, catching and killing small animals and birds. There are five living families of falcon-like birds, including the so-called "true" falcons and the HAWKS.

Falcons have strong, hooked bills. The edges of the bill are notched. They eat insects as well as small animals.

Falcons are found in all parts of the world. Species found in America are duck hawks, pigeon hawks, sparrow hawks and prairie falcons.

The American duck hawk is very swift. It can overtake almost any bird in flight and kill it by striking it to earth with its talons.

Falconry is a sport which dates back to ancient times. The females, usually of the Old World species, were trained to hunt and kill small animals.       I. H. S.

The duck hawk, or peregrine falcon, like all other falcons, is identified by its sharp-pointed wings and long tail

**Fall** see Seasons

**Falling bodies** From the standpoint of common reason and observations made daily, it might seem as though a body which is light in weight would fall more slowly than one which is heavier. This was commonly considered to be the case until about 1590, when GALILEO performed his famous experiment from the Leaning Tower of Pisa. He demonstrated that objects of different weight, dropped from the same height, took the same amount of time to reach the ground.

His experiments were scoffed at for some time because it looked obvious that it took longer for a feather to fall from the same height than it did for an iron ball. However, the real reason it takes longer has nothing to do with the weight of the body or the attraction due to GRAVITY. The frictional effects of air play quite an important role in the length of time the body takes to reach the ground. In comparison to the weight of the feather, the frictional force is quite great but in comparison to the weight of the ball the force is quite small. Actually, if the frictional effects of air resistance could be eliminated, the two bodies would reach the ground in the same amount of time.

A. E. L.

SEE ALSO: ACCELERATION, FRICTION

**Falling star** see Meteor

**Fallopian tubes** see Estrous cycle, Menstruation, Reproductive systems

**Fallout** When a hydrogen bomb is exploded near the ground, thousands of tons of dust and debris are sucked up into the air in a mushroom cloud. These tiny radioactive particles are known as "fallout." Most of the particles settle to the ground near the origin of the blast, but others can be blown hundreds of miles.

SEE: BOMBS; RADIATION; RADIATION, BIOLOGICAL EFFECTS OF

**Fallow** (FAL-oh) Fallow describes land which is plowed and left unplanted for a season or more. This is done for the purpose of freeing fertilizing elements and admitting air into the soil.

SEE: CULTIVATION, NITROGEN CYCLE

**Family** see Animals, classification of; Plants, classification of

**Fang** see Snakes

**Farad** (FAHR-ahd) A farad (f) is a unit of electrical capacitance. A condenser (or capacitor) has a capacitance of one farad when a charge of one COULOMB produces a voltage of one VOLT across its terminals. The unit in common use is the *microfarad,* one-millionth of a farad.

SEE: ELECTRICITY, MEASUREMENT

Michael Faraday and his induction coil

**Faraday, Michael** (1791–1867) Michael Faraday was an English physicist who discovered the laws of electromagnetism. Those laws, in addition to his discoveries of ELECTROLYSIS, are found in every physics textbook. His work in the field of ELECTRICITY made possible the electric light, the electric motor, and the DYNAMO. Without these devices, modern life could not exist.

When Michael was five years old, the Faraday family moved from Newington, Surrey, where Mr. Faraday was a blacksmith, to London. Life was painfully hard for the family, and Michael's share of bread given him from a relief line had to last him one week. "My education," he wrote, "was of the most ordinary description, consisting of little more than the rudiments of reading, writing, and arithmetic at a common day-school. My hours out of school were passed at home (the upper story of an old coach house) or on the streets." But Michael was ambitious. He found a job as errand boy for a bookseller and bookbinder. A year later he was made an apprentice.

He enjoyed his work primarily because it afforded him an opportunity to learn. The three books that introduced him to natural science and electricity were the *Encyclopaedia Britannica,* Watt's *Improvement of the Mind,* and Mrs. Marcet's *Conversations on Chemistry*.

With what money he could spare, Faraday bought materials for experiments, and by 1812 was investigating electrolytic DE-COMPOSITION. That spring a generous customer enabled him to attend four lectures by Sir Humphry Davy at the Royal Institution. He took careful notes, wrote them out in detail, and sent them to Davy with a request for employment at the Institution in any capacity connected with science. Davy suggested that he consider seriously before giving up the security of his trade for the insecurity of science, but when Faraday insisted, Davy hired him as a laboratory assistant. In March, 1813, he became Davy's assistant and accompanied him on a two-year tour of European universities. Many of the important men he met later became his friends and colleagues.

Upon his return to England and the Royal Institution, Faraday began research of his own, continuing as Davy's assistant. He experimented in the fields of electricity and chemistry, becoming an outstanding lecturer and earning honorary degrees and awards from all parts of the world. Faraday's services were eagerly sought by businesses everywhere for fabulous sums of money, but he preferred to remain in the field of scientific research. When he was sixty-seven years old, Queen Victoria provided him with a small pension and a house where he lived the last nine years of his life.      D. H. J.

SEE ALSO: DAVY, SIR HUMPHRY

**Farm** see Agriculture

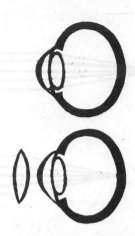

In farsightedness, light rays are focused behind the retina of the eye. A lens corrects this

**Farsightedness** Farsightedness is a condition of faulty vision. The farsighted person can see a long distance, but nearer objects, or those within the usual range, are not so clear. About twenty people out of every hundred are farsighted. When the condition is severe or complicated by other EYE changes, it has to be corrected by glasses.

The basic cause of farsightedness is a variation in the structure of the eye itself, although this is not noticeable to others. The eyeball is not spherical but is shortened. This causes the light rays to come to a FOCUS behind the retina in the back part of the eye. It is stimulation of the cells of the retina which carry the "sight" message to the brain.

The new-born baby and the very young are inclined to farsightedness. This is not usually troublesome because the muscles encircling the lens can contract or relax, changing the shape of the lens slightly. When the lens becomes thicker, the light passing through it is focused more accurately on the retina, overcoming the tendency to have the focus fall behind the retina.

As one reaches middle life, the muscles and other eye structures, particularly the lens, become less elastic. When this happens, the eye loses its ability to accommodate itself to changing conditions, and the person is permanently farsighted.      H. K. S.

SEE ALSO: OPTOMETRY

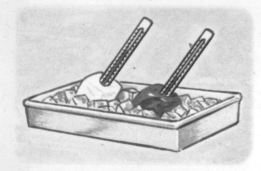

1 Purchase a two-inch cube of suet (fat) and a cube exactly the same size of lean meat. Leave them out of the refrigerator for at least half a day.
2 Check two thermometers for accuracy before beginning the experiment.
3 Insert one thermometer into the cube of fat so the metal tip reaches the center. Push the second thermometer into the cube of meat.
4 Set all of this into a refrigerator or pack in ice and check the temperature every ten minutes. Which tissue, the fat or muscle, gets colder faster?
5 After an hour bring both thermometers and cubes out at room temperature. Which one warms up faster?
6 Can you see why it is advantageous for a whale to have a thick layer of blubber (fat) under its skin?

**Fat** Fat is a fuel food. It is found in cream, butter, the yolk of an egg, meat, gravy, salad dressing, and other foods.

Animals use fat as fuel, as they do CARBOHYDRATES. From these two basic foods—fats and carbohydrates—come the chief sources of energy. Fat yields twice as much energy or heat as carbohydrates. Carbohydrates can be changed into fat and stored.

Carbohydrates are used for quick energy. The body stores fat to be drawn upon when carbohydrates are no longer entering the system through the intestines.

The fat deposits under the skin act as insulation. Fat is a poor conductor of heat and aids in conserving body temperatures. Fat also protects to a degree against injury to deeper parts of the body.

Fats are the same as fixed oils. When an OIL is solid, it is called fat. Examples are lard, tallow (candles, soap), oleomargarine, and even some PLASTICS (which have esters in them).

Every fat has a MELTING POINT at which it will turn into oil. In the same way oil will solidify as it gets cool. Fats in body tissues are mostly the kind with melting points below body temperature.                    B. J. C.
SEE ALSO: ESTER, TALLOW

**Fat, adipose tissue** (ADD-uh-pohs) Fat is a change in, or modification of, fibrous connective tissue. Some of the cells found among the fibers of CONNECTIVE TISSUE begin to store fat. In the beginning small drops of fat appear in the cytoplasm of these cells. As the drops of fat increase in size, they touch one another and unite (*coalesce*) to form larger and larger drops until the whole center of the cell is occupied by one large drop of fat. This is like the way two touching drops of water unite to form a larger drop. The usual parts of the cell are pushed out of the way and stretch out around the edges of the fat drop.

After many fat cells have been formed, the connective tissue seems less dense as its fibers are pushed aside to make room for them. Large numbers of fat cells become so closely packed together that they lose their round or spherical shape. A mass of them looks somewhat like a honeycomb.

An animal that is starving, or one that is hibernating, uses its fat tissue for a source of energy. When the stored fat has been used, the cells return to normal size and appearance.                              J. C. K.
SEE ALSO: CELL, FAT, HIBERNATION, OBESITY

**Fathometer** see Depth sounding

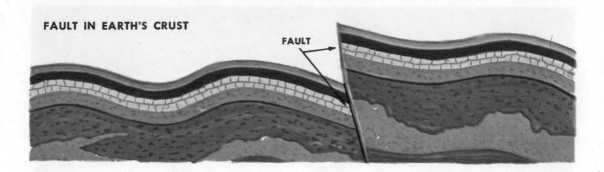

**FAULT IN EARTH'S CRUST**

FAULT

**Fatigue** (fuh-TEEG) Fatigue is a feeling of tiredness which may be caused by physical and mental work, fear, lack of good food, or illness.

The junction of the nerves and muscles, where the nerve impulses are relayed, tires very easily.

· LACTIC ACID and other metabolic waste products accumulate and a decrease in the nutritive material occurs around the muscle or nerve. After resting, the body is again able to dispose of these waste products.

Prolonged fatigue will cause exhaustion and poor health. Sleep or rest will cure most cases of fatigue not due to illness.    B. J. C.

**Fatty acids** Fatty acids are the main ingredients of fats, oils, and waxes. Before fats can be used as food inside the body, the fatty acids must be chemically separated, by digestion, from the glycerol to which they are joined. This same separation occurs when fats become rancid (sour). The odor of rancid fat is the odor of free fatty acids.

The most common fatty acids are *stearic acid,* contained in large amounts in animal fats, and *palmitic* and *oleic* acids, which are found in almost all fats. The saturated fatty acids, and hard animal fats, and processed (hydrogenated) fats are thought harmful to the body when taken in large amounts. They are believed to be a basic cause of hardening of the blood vessels (ARTERIOSCLEROSIS). Unsaturated fatty acids, such as the oils of fish and plants, are essential to the body and are much better food. Fatty acids are also used to make soaps, detergents, paints and resins.    J. K. L.

SEE ALSO: FAT, METABOLISM

**Faulting** A fault is a break or fracture in the earth's crust which causes the layers of earth or rock on one side of the break to be higher than those on the other side. Some MOUNTAINS are formed by faulting.

SEE: EARTHQUAKE, GEOLOGY

**Fauna** (FAW-nuh) Fauna is the animal population of a particular place or of a certain period of time. The term usually covers all animals of a given region during a geological period.

SEE: GEOGRAPHY, GEOLOGIC TIME TABLE, PALEONTOLOGY

**Fawn** see Deer family

Three types of feathers

CONTOUR FEATHER    DOWN    FILO-PLUME    (ENLARGED)

**Feather** Feathers make up the covering of the body and wings of birds. Although feathers are small and light, they protect BIRDS from cold and rain.

Feathers are the outgrowth of the bird's skin. When a feather is fully grown, it is a nonliving structure.

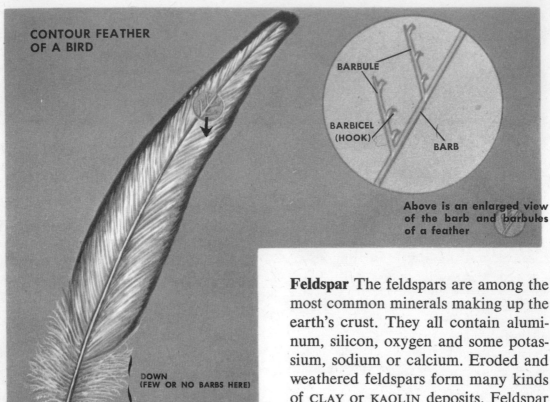

CONTOUR FEATHER OF A BIRD

BARBULE

BARBICEL (HOOK)

BARB

Above is an enlarged view of the barb and barbules of a feather

DOWN (FEW OR NO BARBS HERE)

QUILL

CALAMUS

There are three main types of feathers. *Contour* feathers are large and include wing and tail feathers. *Down,* the softest kind of feathers, grows beneath the contour feathers. Ducks and geese have a padlike covering of down on their bodies. *Filoplumes* are hairlike feathers scattered over the skin between the other feathers.

Each feather has a center *spine* or *shaft.* Arranged along the shaft are small, parallel barbs from which grow *barbules.* The barbules are edged with tiny hooks, *barbicels,* which interlock with those of adjacent barbules, forming a mat-like surface. The barbs at the base have no hooks. The base of the feather is called a *quill.* The part attached to the skin is called a *calamus.*

The dull color of feathers is formed by a color pigment called *melanin.* Bright colors are formed by a substance called *lipochrome.* Iridescent colors are caused by the interference of light waves reflected through colorless filmlike layers of certain barbules. Color seen in soap bubbles and oil film is based on the same principle.      I. H. S.

SEE ALSO: SKIN MODIFICATIONS

**Feldspar** The feldspars are among the most common minerals making up the earth's crust. They all contain aluminum, silicon, oxygen and some potassium, sodium or calcium. Eroded and weathered feldspars form many kinds of CLAY or KAOLIN deposits. Feldspar minerals have wide uses in making pottery glazes and GLASS.

Feldspars occur in mining quantities in about one-sixth of the American states. The coarsely crystalline *pegmatite* rocks are good sources of industrial ceramic grades. Semiprecious varieties of feldspar include pale-blue *amazonstone* and *moonstone.*

Some feldspar crystals occur in lopsided box shapes

The two main types of feldspar are difficult to tell apart. The *orthoclases* contain potassium and the *alkali feldspars* or *plagioclases* contain varying amounts of sodium and calcium.      D. A. B.

**Female** see Heredity

**Femur** see Skeleton

**Fen** see Marsh

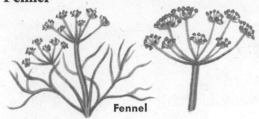
Fennel

**Fennel** (FENN-uhl) Fennel is a plant which belongs to the CARROT family. The seeds are used as a spice in cooking. Fennel grows in all parts of the world. It is a native of lands around the Mediterranean Sea.

The leaves are small and lacy. Fennel bears small yellow flowers. The fruits grow in clusters and hold tiny seeds.

In flavor, the fennel seed is sweet and resembles ANISE. It is used in Italian cookery and French cooks use it on bread and rolls. Fennel is also used to flavor candy, desserts, and soup. The oil of fennel is used in medicine, soaps and perfume. I. H. S.

**Fer de lance** see Snakes

**Fermentation** Fermentation is the oxidation of ORGANIC COMPOUNDS in the absence of gaseous oxygen. It may be done by certain living organisms (YEAST, BACTERIA, MOLD) or by ENZYMES.

**Fermi, Enrico** (FERR-me, en-REE-koh) (1901-1954) Fermi was an Italian physicist who investigated the basic structure of the atomic nucleus. He received the 1938 Nobel Prize for physics for making a new radioactive element by neutron bombardment.

He was a pioneer in the study of nuclear fission (breaking of atoms into parts). He was largely responsible for the achievement of the nuclear chain reaction on December 2, 1942, at the University of Chicago, which made possible the first atomic bomb.

Born in Rome, Fermi studied and taught in Italy. He earned his doctorate from the University of Pisa and later taught at the universities of Florence and Rome, where he made his NOBEL PRIZE discovery. After receiving the Prize in Stockholm, he came to the United States instead of returning to Fascist-controlled Italy. He was professor of physics at Columbia University before he came to the University of Chicago to work on the atomic pile. He then became associate director of Los Alamos Laboratory, where the atomic bombs were tested. In 1946, he received the Congressional Medal for Merit and returned to Chicago as a member of the Institute for Basic Research. C. L. K.

Fermi was largely responsible for the first controlled nuclear chain reaction. It took place on December 2, 1942, at Stagg Field of the University of Chicago

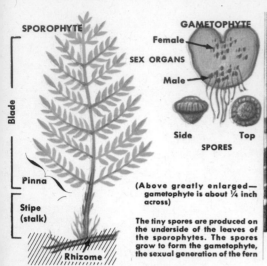

SPOROPHYTE

Blade

Pinna

Stipe (stalk)

Rhizome

GAMETOPHYTE

Female

SEX ORGANS

Male

Side     Top

SPORES

(Above greatly enlarged—gametophyte is about ¼ inch across)

The tiny spores are produced on the underside of the leaves of the sporophytes. The spores grow to form the gametophyte, the sexual generation of the fern

FERNS

Some ferns living today are similar to their ancestors that lived millions of years ago

**Fermium** Fermium is a chemical element. It is one of the RARE-EARTH elements. It was discovered in 1952. Unmanned airplanes traveled through the radioactive clouds created by an H-bomb explosion. Material in the clouds was gathered by the airplanes. It was brought back to be examined. A new element was discovered in it.

After having been discovered, fermium was later made in a cyclotron and in a reactor. The Argonne Laboratory, Los Alamos Laboratory, and the University of California are credited with its discovery.

The symbol for fermium is Fm. It is a radioactive element in the ACTINIDE SERIES. Its chemical properties are similar to those of ERBIUM. The atomic number of fermium is 100. The mass number of its most stable isotope is 253.     D. E. Z.

SEE ALSO: ATOM, ELEMENTS

**Ferns** Ferns are members of the highest division of the plant kingdom. These plants, with their well-developed roots, and efficient water and food conducting systems, have become an important plant in many parts of the earth. Ferns grow in a variety of places, but most species prefer a moist, shady habitat.

Ferns are usually PERENNIAL with horizontal, underground stems—*rhizomes*—which develop new fronds each year. The young leaves unroll at the tip, making the young plant look much like the head of a fiddle. The veins of the leaves branch into two almost equal forks which may unite to form a network of veins. The leaves are usually very irregular in outline, although, in a few species, they may be more regular.

Asexual reproduction in ferns is by SPORE FORMATION. These may develop on a separate frond, *sporophyll,* or they may be on the under side of regular leaves. Spores are produced in organs (*sporangia*) which are clustered together in groups known as *sori.* When a spore germinates it produces a *gametophyte* (the sexual generation). This is a small, flattened, heart-shaped structure which bears the male and female sex organs, *antheridia* and *archegonia.* When the moisture is right, the mature antheridia rupture, permitting the motile sperm cells to swim into the archegonia to fertilize the egg cells. The sporophyte generation develops from the fertilized egg.

Like the MOSSES, the ferns are excellent examples of the ALTERNATION OF GENERATIONS. In the ferns, however, the sporophyte is the important and familiar generation.

Ferns are a very old group of plants dating back to the Devonian period. They were the dominant plants of the MESOZOIC ERA. However, today the seed plants are more important.     M. D. F.

SEE ALSO: PLANTS, CLASSIFICATION OF

**Ferret** see Weasel

**Fertile** see Nuclear science glossary

# ☀ THINGS TO DO

## GROWING TWO GENERATIONS OF THE FERN CYCLE

1. The fern (sporophyte generation) will thrive well in a bog terrarium. (See the Terrarium article for making it.)

2. Have the new home established before you go fern hunting. Ferns are found in wooded areas along the banks of streams or in a marshy environment.

3. Dig up the plant, being sure the entire underground stem is taken with it. Wrap it in wet newspaper and transfer the plants to the terrarium.

4. Keep the terrarium in a north window and water frequently.

5. To grow the second generation, the gametophyte, wait until the spores appear on the underside of the fronds. Tap the compound leaf over a sheet of paper and the spores will fall off.

6. Fill a pot with soil and peat moss. Put a layer of sand on top.

7. Pour boiling water over the whole mixture and the container to destroy any bacteria or mold spores which will attack the germinating fern spores, and let it cool.

8. Sprinkle the spores on the sand, cover the pot with clear glass, and set the pot in a saucer in order to water from the bottom.

9. In several weeks the spores will develop into minute heart-shaped gametophyte plants. This plant produces eggs and sperms. When a sperm fertilizes an egg, a small fern sporophyte will grow out of this plant. When it is several inches tall transfer it to the bog terrarium.

**Fertilization** Fertilization is the union of male and female gametes (the sperm and egg) to form a single cell from which a new individual develops.
SEE: EMBRYOLOGY, REPRODUCTIVE SYSTEMS

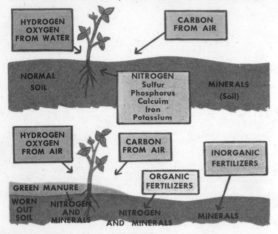

HYDROGEN OXYGEN FROM WATER

CARBON FROM AIR

NORMAL SOIL

NITROGEN Sulfur Phosphorus Calcium Iron Potassium

MINERALS (Soil)

HYDROGEN OXYGEN FROM AIR

CARBON FROM AIR

INORGANIC FERTILIZERS

ORGANIC FERTILIZERS

GREEN MANURE

WORN OUT SOIL

NITROGEN AND MINERALS

NITROGEN AND MINERALS

MINERALS

Fertilizers put food for plants back in the soil

**Fertilizer** Fertilizers are used to put more plant food into soil. All plants need a balanced food supply in order to develop properly. When the same crop is planted in the same field every year, it uses up much of the food in the soil, and the land is said to be "worn out." Fertilizers put plant food back into the soil. Different crops should be planted in the field each season. This is called *crop rotation*.

Plants need many elements—oxygen, hydrogen, carbon, nitrogen, sulfur, phosphorus, calcium, iron, potassium, and magnesium—in order to live. CARBON DIOXIDE in the air provides the carbon, and water supplies hydrogen and oxygen. The rest must be supplied through the soil.

There are three main kinds of fertilizers: organic, inorganic, and green manure. *Organic fertilizers* consist of manure and fish and bone meal. They supply nitrogen. The *inorganic* or *chemical* fertilizers contain minerals which are mined. Fertilizer known as *green manure* or *cover crop* is provided by planting a crop of some plant, such as ALFALFA, which stores nitrogen from the air. A crop such as CLOVER or cowpeas is raised and then plowed under. M. R. L.
SEE ALSO: AGRICULTURE, NITROGEN CYCLE

**Fetus** (FEE-tuhs) A fetus is an unborn mammal in the last stages of development within the mother's body. In man, the new individual, or baby, is classed as an embryo for the first three months of existence in the uterus. It is a fetus from then until born.
SEE: EMBRYOLOGY, MAMMALIA, PREGNANCY

**Fever** When the temperature of the body of man rises above the normal temperature of 98.6 degrees Fahrenheit, fever is present. It is a symptom of infection in the body. The heat of fever is one of the methods the body uses to help overcome the infection.

Loss of appetite and a chill usually accompany the beginning of a fever. As the temperature rises, the patient becomes hot and thirsty and many have a headache. Pathologists consider the rising fever to be the result of toxins of the infection acting on the heat centers of the brain. As the infection subsides, the body temperature returns to normal and the patient rests more easily. Fever can often be reduced with ASPIRIN, but the infection causing it should be treated by a physician. P. G. B.
SEE ALSO: MEDICINE, PATHOLOGY

**Fiber** A fiber is a thin thread-like strand. In plants, it is either a thin root or a long thin cell. In animals, a fiber is a long, thin strand which makes up part of the CONNECTIVE TISSUE, MUSCLE TISSUE, and nerve tissues in the body.
SEE: ECONOMIC BOTANY, NERVE CELL

**Fibrin and fibrinogen** see Blood, Circulatory system

Enlargements of wool fibers (left) and cotton fibers (right)

Photo-micrograph by National Teaching Aids, Inc.

Yellow elastic fibers in the trachea intertwine. The cells lie outside the fibers. The magnified cross-section (left) shows: A—air passage; B—lining; C—fibrous tissue; D—cartilage ring

**Fibrous tissue** Fibrous tissue helps to hold the internal organs and bones in place. It is a type of CONNECTIVE TISSUE. Fibrous tissue is made of white or yellow fibers and scattered cells. The cells make the fibers which are laid down outside the cell bodies.

The *yellow* elastic fibers are usually found where there is continuous but varying STRESS. Numerous branching yellow elastic fibers lie parallel to each other or interlace with each other. This kind of fibrous tissue is found in the walls of the air tubes (RESPIRATORY SYSTEM) and in the vocal cords.

The stronger *white* fibers predominate where great strength and flexibility are required. The white fibers are found in *ligaments* which attach bones to bones and in *tendons* which attach muscles to bones. The fibers may be arranged in parallels, as in tendons, or interlaced in a membrane as in the ligament covering JOINTS.

When ligaments are torn, a "sprain" results. If, in addition, the bone becomes dislodged and imbedded in the muscle, a "dislocation" is suffered.

The Achilles tendon attaching the calf muscle of the leg to the heel is called this because Achilles, the mythical hero, was held by the heels when dipped in the river Styx to make him invulnerable. Later a wound in the heel killed him.

The white fibers are largely made of *collagen* which, on being boiled with dilute acid, is transformed into gelatin. The yellow fibers contain the protein *elastin*. E. M. S.

SEE ALSO: HISTOLOGY, MUSCLE TISSUE, SKELETON

**Fibula** see Skeleton

**Field, Cyrus West** (1819–1892) Cyrus Field was an American businessman who, in 1854, organized the New York, Newfoundland and London Telegraph Company to lay a trans-Atlantic cable. After three unsuccessful attempts, the cable was finally laid in July, 1866.

Cyrus Field was born in Stockbridge, Massachusetts, on November 30, 1819. At the age of fifteen he went to New York City and found a job as an errand boy in a dry goods store. After working briefly as an assistant to his brother Matthew, a paper manufacturer, in 1841 he organized his own business, the Cyrus W. Field and Company of New York, wholesale paper dealers.

In 1854 he organized the New York, Newfoundland and London Telegraph Company, and formed a similar company in Great Britain. The purpose of these two companies was to lay a cable across the Atlantic Ocean. A complete cable was laid between July 7 and August 5, 1858 and operated for three weeks. Queen Victoria sent a TELEGRAPH message across the Atlantic to President James Buchanan, and the world rejoiced. However, the insulation failed and the project had to be abandoned.

In 1866 Field chartered the *Great Eastern,* and finally laid a successful cable. He was awarded a gold medal by Congress, and he received many honors.

During the last twenty-seven years of his life Field helped lay submarine cables to other parts of the world. He also became interested in the New York Elevated Railroad Company. He served as president for three years, and then turned his interest in organization to the Wabash Railroad. D. H. J.

**Fig** 680 **Filbert**

**Fig tree and varieties of the fruit**

**Fig** The fig is a small tree or shrub which has been grown for over 4000 years. It originally came from Arabia. The pear-shaped fruit is not the true fruit of the tree. It is a hollow receptacle that is the swollen upper end of the flower stalk. Tiny flowers line the inside of this structure. They develop into small fruits called *achenes*.

There are several species of figs. The *golden fig* is an epiphyte. It starts its growth on another tree, sends out air roots, and finally grows downward until it anchors itself into the soil. During this process the host tree dies.

The *San Pedro fig* is grown in California and two crops of fruit are produced each year. The *common fig* lacks male flowers so the fruit matures seedless. Development of fruit without POLLINATION is called *parthenocarpy*.

Until the fruit growers in California learned about a particular *fig wasp,* they had little success raising the *Smyrna fig.* This tree has only female flowers. It needs the small female wasp which inhabits fruit of the wild *caprifig.* The insect carries the pollen from a male flower on this species to the female flower on the Smyrna fig. This process is called *caprification.* H. J. C.

**Filaria** (fih-LAIR-ee-uh) A filaria is a long thread-like worm. It lives in the bodies of other animals. This means it is a *parasite*. The adults are found in the tissues of vertebrate animals. After the larvae develop, they cannot become adults unless part of their lives are spent within the bodies of insects. Most filariae are found in tropical countries.

One species of filaria lives in the lymph glands of man and may produce a disease called *elephantiasis*. It is so named because in a heavy infection (infestation) the arms, legs and other parts of the body swell to an enormous size. This probably happens because the lymph passages become blocked.

This species has an interesting life cycle. The adult worms are two to four inches long and they live inside human beings. The females give birth to tiny larvae so small that one must view them under a microscope. After birth, the larvae find their way into the blood stream of man. During the day they live in the lungs and larger blood vessels. At night they migrate (move) to the blood vessels of the skin. This increases their chances of being sucked up by night-feeding mosquitos. It is interesting that in places where the mosquitos feed during the day, the time of the larva's day-night migration is reversed. Unless they are sucked up by such mosquitos, the larvae cannot live.

Once inside the mosquito, the larvae pass from its stomach to its muscles where they change (metamorphose) and increase in size, before migrating back to the sucking tube (proboscis). When a person is bitten by an infected mosquito, the larvae enter the bloodstream of that person. They then pass to the lymph vessels and glands. There they coil up and mature into adults and the whole cycle starts again. I. H. S.

SEE ALSO: METAMORPHOSIS

**Filbert** see Nuts

**Filariae**

**Progressive enlargements of a photographic film negative**

The original negative

Enlarged 25 times

Enlarged 250 times—
silver grains show

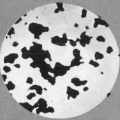
Undeveloped grains
in an emulsion

2,500 times—
grains are growing

25,000 times—
grains become fibers

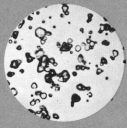
Developed grains
in an emulsion

**Film** Film is a plastic-like material in thin sheets used for taking photographs. It is coated with special chemicals which are sensitive to light. These chemicals form an EMULSION, made up of gelatin and crystals of SILVER salts.

The process of film-making is an interesting one. The most important chemical used in the first step toward making film is silver nitrate. By placing silver ingots in nitric acid, the metal and acid combine and form crystals of silver nitrate.

The next step in the film preparation is to make an emulsion of silver bromide and gelatin. Silver nitrate, gelatin, and potassium bromide are mixed together in water. The potassium bromide and silver nitrate combine. Crystals of silver bromide are left in the gelatin. These particles are very sensitive to light and separate when light strikes them. When processed, this produces a *negative* which shows everything dark where the original scene was light, and light where everything was dark. Now the emulsion is complete and ready for use.

A film base must be prepared on which the emulsion will form a coating. Wood pulp or cotton is treated with ACETIC ACID to form cellulose acetate. It is then dissolved in a solvent and becomes a thick fluid which is called "dope." During a heating process the "dope" is turned into a very thin sheet. It is now transparent and ready to be coated with the emulsion. After coating, it is wound on metal spools and then packaged for sale.

Amateur photographers like to develop their own film into "positive" prints. Because the film is so light-sensitive, it must be developed in a completely dark room. The papers used for prints are coated with an emulsion quite like the one used on the film. After the print paper is placed against the negative under a white light, the print is then put through special chemical solutions and the image that appears has reproduced the lights and darks exactly as they were in the original scene photographed.

Color films reproduce a subject in its true life colors—red, green, and blue—from which all other colors come. There is also an emulsion backing on the film. When the pictures are developed, they are seen in the complementary colors which are exactly like those of the original subject.    D. A. B.

SEE ALSO: CAMERA, PHOTOGRAPHY

**Filter** A filter is any object that can stop the passage of certain parts of a substance, while it lets the rest of the substance pass through it. A sieve is a filter. Sand and CHARCOAL are filters often used to remove impurities from drinking water.

In PHYSICS, a filter is a device that stops certain waves or rays (of sound, COLOR, or electricity) and lets others through.

SEE: CHEMISTRY, PURIFICATION, SOUND

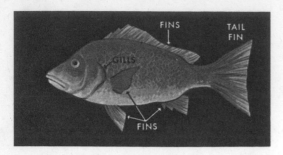

**Fin** A fin is the membranous organ attached to the body of a FISH. It corresponds to wings or limbs in other animals. It is used for locomotion, steering and balance in the water.

SEE: PISCES

**Finch** Finch refers not to one particular bird as does the word *American robin,* for example, but to a large group of birds known as *seed-eaters.* Some of the common birds which belong to this group are buntings, grosbeaks, sparrows, kingbirds, canaries and bullfinches.

Being seed eaters, finches have bills which are adapted for obtaining and cracking seeds. Generally they are cone-shaped and sharply pointed, small in juncos or canaries, and very heavy in grosbeaks and cardinals. In the CROSSBILL the tip is crossed.

Many of the finches are fairly drab in appearance. However some are highly colorful and often have beautiful songs, as for example the GOLDFINCH, CANARY, bullfinch, grosbeak and CARDINAL.

Finches are found in all parts of the world except the Australian region. The finch family contains about 500 species, a very large group.     D. J. I.

**Grosbeak**

**Purple finch**

**English sparrow**

**Fiord** (FYOHRD) A long narrow, steep-sided inlet of a sea is called a fiord. Some fiords are as long as one hundred miles with sides 4000 feet deep. The shallowest part of the fiord is at its mouth—the deepest part always some distance from the sea.

Fiords are found in plateau areas of Alaska, Scotland, Ireland, Antarctica, Norway, British Columbia and New Zealand. The name "fiord" (sometimes spelled "fjord") applies chiefly to those in Norway. In Scotland, they are called *firths* or *sea lochs.*

Fiords were formed by the action of GLACIERS which scooped out valleys in resistant rock layers. Drowned river valleys, as in Ireland, are not true fiords.     J. A. D.

SEE ALSO: GEOLOGY, RIVER

**A fiord**
Courtesy Society For Visual Education, Inc.

American Forest Products Industries, Inc.
**Douglas fir, a false hemlock**

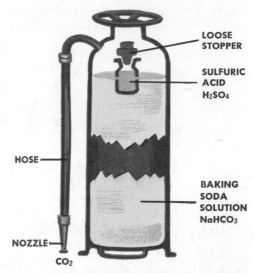

**Cut-away of a soda-acid fire extinguisher**

**Fir** Fir is any tree of the many cone-bearing, resinous, pyramid-shaped evergreens. The Norway SPRUCE fir can reach a height of over 150 feet. A well-known American species is the BALSAM fir. Because the wood is light, soft, and not strong, it is usually used to finish interiors and to make boxes.
SEE: PINE, TREE

**Fire** When enough heat, fuel, and oxygen are present, a fire results. If any of these three things are lacking, there can be no fire. If any of the three are removed from a fire, it will stop burning and go out.

Fire is a chemical change that releases two kinds of ENERGY—heat and light. The release of energy takes place when the materials or some of the materials in the fuel combine with oxygen and form new materials.

Fires have always been very useful and necessary but can also be very destructive and harmful.                                    J. D. B.
SEE ALSO: COMBUSTION, FIRE EXTINGUISHER, OXIDATION

If any of the three components is removed, a fire cannot continue

HEAT FUEL
OXYGEN

**Fire extinguisher** A fire extinguisher is a metal container which usually holds chemicals for putting out fires. When the chemicals mix and are sprayed on a fire, the fire goes out quickly. Fire extinguishers must be cleaned and inspected often, so they will be ready for use in case of an emergency.

The most widely used fire extinguisher is the *soda-acid* type. It contains a solution of bicarbonate of soda and water. There is a small bottle of SULFURIC ACID inside. To use the extinguisher one must turn it upside down. The stopper inside the sulfuric acid bottle comes loose. The acid pours out of the bottle and mixes with the chemicals to form CARBON DIOXIDE ($CO_2$). This carbon dioxide gas forces the chemicals through a hose attached to the container. It can then be sprayed onto the fire.

Another well-known extinguisher is the *foam* type. This is used mainly on gasoline or oil fires, because the foam smothers the flames of a burning liquid. These fire extinguishers contain a solution of SODIUM BICARBONATE in one compartment and aluminum sulfate in another. When the extinguisher is inverted, the solutions mix into a foam which is forced through a hose.

A third type is a tank of carbon dioxide under pressure. When released, the $CO_2$ cuts off the oxygen supply to the fire and it cannot continue burning.

## ✳ THINGS TO DO

### MAKING A FIRE EXTINGUISHER

**Materials: A pop bottle, soda straw, soda, vinegar, and clay.**

1   Form the clay around the end of the straw into a plug which can be used to cap the bottle. Fill the pop bottle half full of vinegar. Drop a tablespoon of baking soda into the bottle and immediately cap it with the clay-straw plug.

2   Have a small paper fire burning on a cookie sheet. Tilt the bottle, aiming the straw at the flames. What happened to the fire?

3   When vinegar and soda are combined a chemical change releases carbon dioxide. This gas is heavier than air, does not support combustion, and will smother the blaze.

*Automatic sprinklers* are frequently used in department stores and factories where large areas must be protected against fires. Pipes which contain water under pressure are placed throughout the ceilings. Sprinkler heads, which have soft metal plugs in them, are set into the pipes every eight to ten feet. If a fire breaks out in a room with such a system, the plugs melt when the heat reaches 165° F. This opens the sprinklers and the water sprays out with great force over the entire area. A bell rings until the water is shut off by the fire department.    J. H. D.

**Firearms** see Weapons

**Firefly** see Beetles

**First aid** The care given to an injured or suddenly ill person before a doctor arrives is first aid. It is given *only* to prevent death or permanent disability. First aid care should not take the place of the doctor.

General directions that should be followed when a person is injured include:

1. A doctor should be called while first aid is being given.
2. The injured person must be kept lying down, his head level with the rest of his body unless he has a head injury. If he has a head injury, his head should be slightly raised.
3. An injured person *should not be moved,* except to remove him from fire, flood, smoke, or anything that would further endanger his life.
4. An injured person should be examined to see if emergency action is really necessary. If he is *not* in danger of bleeding to death, or is *not* suffocating, or has *not* been severely burned, or is *not* in shock, the untrained person should leave him alone.
5. An unconscious or semiconscious person should never be given anything to drink.
6. An injured person should be kept warm—not hot.
7. Other people should be kept away from the injured person.
8. An injured person should be reassured, not permitted to see his wounds, and kept comfortable until a doctor comes.

*Shock* can result from almost any injury. Shock is a slowing down of bodily activity and can result in death. A person in shock

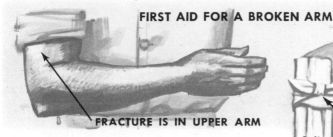

**FIRST AID FOR A BROKEN ARM**

**FRACTURE IS IN UPPER ARM**

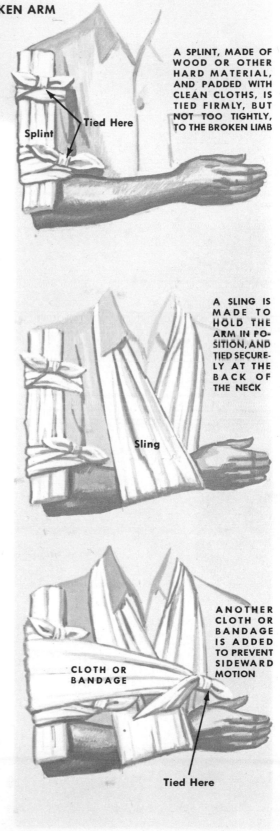

A SPLINT, MADE OF WOOD OR OTHER HARD MATERIAL, AND PADDED WITH CLEAN CLOTHS, IS TIED FIRMLY, BUT NOT TOO TIGHTLY, TO THE BROKEN LIMB

**Tied Here**

**Splint**

A SLING IS MADE TO HOLD THE ARM IN PO-SITION, AND TIED SECURE-LY AT THE BACK OF THE NECK

**Sling**

ANOTHER CLOTH OR BANDAGE IS ADDED TO PREVENT SIDEWARD MOTION

**CLOTH OR BANDAGE**

**Tied Here**

may have a pale face, cold sweat, a weak but rapid pulse, and nausea. His head should be kept level with or lower than his body, except if he has a head injury. He should be kept warm. If the injured person is conscious and does not have an abdominal injury, he should be given plenty of water, with salt and baking soda added.

*Bleeding* can usually be stopped by applying pressure. A clean dressing should be placed over the wound and pressure exerted. When bleeding has been controlled, additional layers of bandage or cloth should be added to keep the original dressing firmly in place. A tourniquet should be used *only* when the person is in danger of death from uncontrolled bleeding.

*Burns* may result in shock and infection. The pain may be relieved by immersing the burned area in cold water. This treatment also seems to lessen somewhat the severity of the burn. Grease, oil, or anything a doctor would have to remove before treating the burn must *never* be used. The burned area may be covered with a clean dry dressing that will not stick.

An ice bag should be applied to the area of a *fracture* to relieve pain. A person with possible fractures should not be moved except to prevent further injury. The broken bone must be splinted before he is moved. A board, a thick bundle of newspapers, or even a pillow can be used. The splint should be tied firmly in place above and below the break. If the neck or back is injured, the victim *must not be moved.*

*Poisoning* requires emergency treatment even before the doctor is called. Except in alkali (such as lye) or kerosene poisoning, the victim must be made to vomit by giving him a salt solution or warm water and mustard. After vomiting, the antidote should be given, if known. If the poison is an acid, the victim should be given baking soda in water and then warm milk. If an alkali poison, the victim should be given lemon juice or vine-

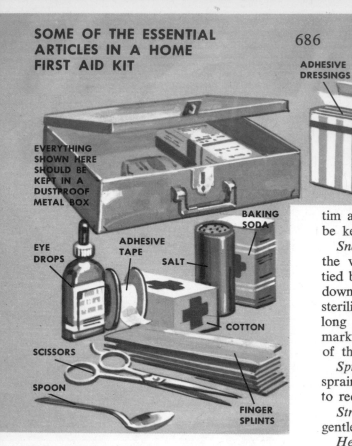

ADHESIVE
DRESSINGS

ROLL OF
GAUZE
BANDAGE

TINCTURE
OF IODINE

WATER-
PURIFYING
TABLETS

EVERYTHING
SHOWN HERE
SHOULD BE
KEPT IN A
DUSTPROOF
METAL BOX

BAKING
SODA

EYE
DROPS

ADHESIVE
TAPE

SALT

COTTON

SCISSORS

SPOON

FINGER
SPLINTS

gar and then some warm milk to drink.

*Suffocation* can result from pressure on the neck or chest, an electric shock, or swallowing liquids, smoke, or, especially in children, small hard objects. The cause of suffocation must first be removed, for example by taking the victim out of a smoke-filled room. ARTIFICIAL RESPIRATION should then be applied until the victim resumes breathing or is pronounced dead. The mouth-to-mouth method of artificial respiration, in which the person applying first aid first blows into and then sucks air out of the victim's mouth, is an easy and very effective method.

*Cuts and lacerations* should be thoroughly cleaned with soap and water. A large cut should be seen by a doctor. Puncture wounds should *always* be seen by a doctor because of the danger of tetanus infections.

*Foreign bodies* in the eye may be washed out with a solution of one teaspoon of baking soda in a glass of warm, sterilized water. Foreign bodies in the nose or ear should be removed by a physician. If the victim is choking due to a foreign body in the throat, he should be turned upside down and slapped on the back.

*Animal bites* should be cleaned with soap and water. A doctor should see the vic-tim as soon as possible. The animal should be kept under observation for rabies.

*Snake bites* require special care. With the victim lying down, a band should be tied between the bite and the heart, to slow down the spread of the poison. Using a sterilized knife, crisscross cuts about ¼ inch long should be made through each fang mark. The venom must then be sucked out of the bite but must be instantly spit out.

*Sprains* may be treated by elevating the sprained area. Ice packs should be applied to reduce pain and swelling.

*Strains* are best treated with heat and gentle massage of the strained muscles.

*Heat exhaustion* can be recognized by a pale, cold skin, profuse perspiration, a weak pulse, weakness, nausea, and dizziness. The victim needs fresh air, treatment for shock, and replacement of the salt that was lost.

*Sunstroke* is characterized by dizziness, nausea, pains in the head, dry skin and mouth, flushed face, high temperature, and a rapid pulse. The victim should lie down with his head elevated and ice bags should be applied.

*Frostbite* victims should be brought indoors and given a warm drink. The frozen area should be thawed in cool water or air. The area surrounding the frostbitten area should be massaged but should *not* be massaged with snow.　　　　J. D. B.

**Fish** Not all the animals that live in water are fish. Tadpoles, frogs, and newts, for instance, spend part of their lives in water. But they are amphibians, not fish. Some snakes and other reptiles live partly in water, too. Seals and whales are warm-blooded mammals. Crayfish, starfish and jellyfish are not true fish. Sharks, lampreys, hagfish, and bony fish are all true fish.

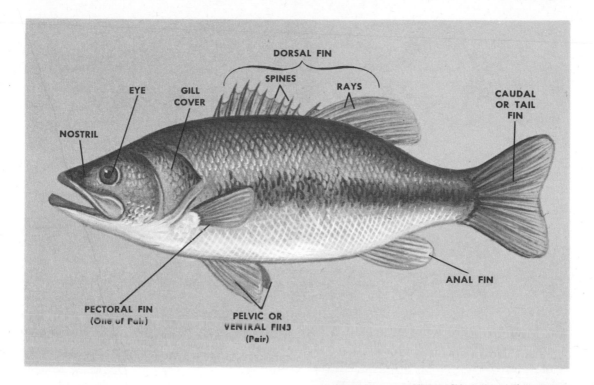

EYE · GILL COVER · NOSTRIL · DORSAL FIN · SPINES · RAYS · CAUDAL OR TAIL FIN · ANAL FIN · PECTORAL FIN (One of Pair) · PELVIC OR VENTRAL FINS (Pair)

1—Fresh water fish in Lake Michigan
2—Marine habitat group off the coast of Texas in the Gulf of Mexico
3—Marine shore group off the Maine coast

All photos Chicago Natural History Museum

"Fish" is a general name that many people give to vertebrates that live in water, breathe through gills, and swim with fins. Modern scientists, however, usually make a separate grouping for the jawless and gill-less fish, such as lampreys and hagfish. These animals look somewhat like eels. This group is called *Agnatha,* or sometimes *Cyclostomata.*

SHARKS and other cartilaginous fish are called *Chondrichthyes.* These animals do not have a true bony skeleton. Their skeletons are made of CARTILAGE, a firm, flexible substance. The cartilaginous group of fish may have a tough skin with toothlike scales. They do not have ribs, lungs, an air bladder, or true gill covers. Their fins are supported by cartilaginous fin rays. Some fish have bony, jointed fin rays.

The differences between cartilaginous fish and bony fish (the *teleosts*) have special significance in evolutionary studies.     C. L. K.

SEE ALSO: PISCES

**Fish hawk** see Osprey

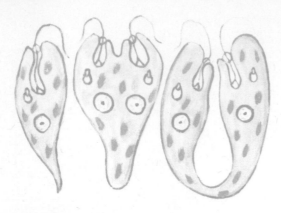

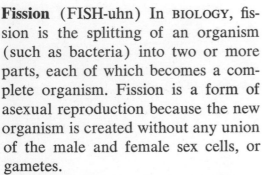

**Fission of Euglena**

**Fittonia**

**Fission** (FISH-uhn) In BIOLOGY, fission is the splitting of an organism (such as bacteria) into two or more parts, each of which becomes a complete organism. Fission is a form of asexual reproduction because the new organism is created without any union of the male and female sex cells, or gametes.

In physics, fission is the splitting of the nucleus of an atom.
SEE: NUCLEAR SCIENCE; REPRODUCTION, ASEXUAL

**Fissionable** see Nuclear science glossary

**Fittonia** (fih-TONE-yuh) Fittonia is a tropical, PERENNIAL plant which is raised mainly for its hairy and beautifully veined foliage. Fittonias will grow in shade and in places that most other plants will not grow. They are useful as low or creeping foliage plants. They should be planted in pots, with equal parts of sand, leaf-mold and loam.

Fittonias have small, two-lipped flowers which are hidden by their leaves. Some fittonias have dark green leaves which are veined with red. Others have white-veined leaves. The largest fittonia is about a foot in height and has red-veined, short-pointed leaves. M. R. L.
SEE ALSO: PLANTS, TROPICAL

**Fjord** see Fiord

**Flagella** (fluh-JELL-uh) In BOTANY, flagella are thin thread-like roots or runners. In BIOLOGY, flagella are whip-like appendages, or parts, on certain organisms (some PROTOZOA and BACTERIA) by which the organism moves.
SEE: ANIMALS, CLASSIFICATION OF

**Flame** see Combustion

**Flamingo** In spite of its deep voice and height of nearly five feet, the flamingo is a very timid bird. Its long legs are like the heron's, but its feet are webbed like a duck's. When feeding, the flamingo buries its curved bill upside down in water or mud. Its food, seeds and small water animals, are strained out by the fine comb-like edges at the side of the bill.

**Flamingos**
Courtesy Society For Visual Education, Inc.

This bird lives along coastal areas or shallow lagoons of tropical regions. At one time, the demand for the beautiful scarlet plumage of the American flamingo nearly caused its extinction. It is now protected by law. In Europe and Africa, the flamingo is usually white. Other species of flamingo may be pink or white with black wing quills.

The flamingo builds its nest of mud, less than a foot high and a foot wide. It lays one or two white eggs in a shallow depression. Both parents share the thirty-day incubation period.                                     J. A. D.

SEE ALSO: BIRD, HERON

**Flatfish** Flatfish are FISH that have compressed, or flat, bodies. As adults, they have both eyes on the same side of the head. The FLOUNDER and HALIBUT are kinds of flatfish.

**Flatworm** see Planaria, Platyhelminthes

**Flax** see Linen

**Flea**

**Flea** The flea is a tiny insect that is smaller than a fraction of an inch, yet can jump nearly fifty times its length. Fleas are wingless. The largest flea is less than one-fourth of an inch in size. A tiny flea can jump nearly thirteen inches. It is a pest because it sucks the blood of mammals and birds and can pass germs from one to the other.

The flea eggs, laid in the feathers or hair of the host, go through complete metamorphosis from egg to adult. This cycle ranges from two weeks to a year depending upon the species. Although they usually feed once a day, some fleas can go without food for several weeks.                          J. A. D.

SEE ALSO: INSECTA, METAMORPHOSIS

**Fleming, Sir Alexander** (1881-1955) Sir Alexander Fleming was the British bacteriologist who discovered the green mold *Penicillium notatum* from which PENICILLIN is made.

Little is known about Dr. Fleming's childhood except that he was born on a farm at Lochfield, Scotland, the seventh of eight children. At fourteen he went to London to live with an older brother, a doctor. He attended Kilmarnock Academy where he won almost all the prizes and scholarships. He then entered St. Mary's Hospital Medical School in London, where he was a brilliant student, earning honors in physiology, pharmacology, medicine, pathology and hygiene.

While a captain in the Royal Air Medical Corps in France during World War I, Fleming discovered that the ANTISEPTICS used to treat wounds actually caused infection. Instead of killing BACTERIA, these antiseptics destroyed the white blood cells and thus deprived the body of one of its main defenses. Dr. Fleming determined to develop a bacteria-fighter harmless to animal tissues.

In 1922, Fleming found "a substance present in the tissues and secretions of the body which is capable of rapidly dissolving certain bacteria." As it resembled an enzyme and was able to *lyse* (dissolve) cells, he called it "lysozyme." Lysozyme is widely used in BACTERIOLOGY.

In 1928, a green mold ruined one of Fleming's bacteria cultures. He found that this mold did not damage the white blood cells of test mice. He had his bacterium-fighter, but medical researchers were more interested in the new SULFA DRUGS. When the inadequacies of sulfa were discovered, Sir Howard Walter Florey, an Oxford University pathologist, remembered Fleming's green mold. With his wife, also a physician, and Dr. Ernst Chain, he developed natural penicillin, the first major ANTIBIOTIC.

For his pioneering work in bacteriology, Fleming was knighted in 1944. He shared the 1945 NOBEL PRIZE for medicine with Sir Howard Florey and Dr. Chain.        D. H. J.

**Flesh** Flesh is the soft part of an animal body, such as muscle, fat, and skin. Animals that eat the flesh of other animals are called *carnivores*.

The flicker is a climbing bird

**Flicker** The flicker is a familiar bird of North America. Its length of thirteen inches makes it one of the larger members of the WOODPECKER family. This bird's call sounds like "flick′-er, flick′-er." Its nest is usually a hole in a post or tree with five to ten white eggs.

The eastern flicker is known as the yellow-shafted or *golden-winged flicker* because of the golden underparts of its wings and tail. Both male and female have the same coloring, but only the male has a black mark or "mustache" beside its beak. Along the Pacific coast, the *red-shafted flicker* is more common. This bird has a red mustache and the underparts of wings and tail are red.

Like most woodpeckers, the flicker has four toes on each foot, two of which point backward. These back-pointed toes and stiff tail feathers brace it as it bores into wood, probing for insects, with its sharp bill. A long sticky tongue also aids it in finding insects on the ground.                    J. A. D.

**Flight, principles of** Through the ages, man has watched the birds and dreamed of flying. In every age "scientists" devised flying machines. The earliest recorded model, based on bird flight, dates back to 400 B.C.

Birds fly by moving their wings down and up. During the downstroke, the wing moves forward and down with a twisting motion. The BIRD then moves forward rapidly. During the upstroke, the wings move backward, but the bird still moves forward because of momentum gained on the downstroke. The tips of the wings move much more rapidly than the point at which they are attached to the body of the bird.

Many of the early flying machines were *ornithopters*. An ornithopter is an aircraft which has wings that try to duplicate the movement of those of a bird in flight. Although small-scale models have been built and flown successfully, the mechanical problems in making the conversion from a model to a full-size aircraft have not been solved.

### LIFT AND GRAVITY

The wings of fixed-wing aircraft are shaped so that air flowing over the top of the wing moves faster than air moving across the bottom. The faster moving air has less pressure, and the greater pressure on the bottom of the wing makes it rise. This upward push is called *lift*.

Lift may be increased by increasing the speed of the aircraft or the angle at which the wing is moved through the air. This *angle of attack* is increased by raising the nose of the aircraft. If the angle of attack becomes too great, the flow of air over the top of the wing will start to swirl and burble, causing a loss of lift called a *stall*. The angle of attack must then be reduced, and the speed of the wing through the air increased, to restore the lift necessary to maintain flight.

Most aircraft have *flaps*, trailing edge sections of their wings hinged to lower downward. This changes the shape of the wing airfoil to provide greater lift at low speeds for safer take-offs and landings.

Lift must be greater than the force of *gravity* acting upon the aircraft for it to leave the ground and climb into the atmosphere. In straight and level flight, lift and gravity are in exact balance. When gravity is greater than lift, the aircraft will descend.

### THRUST AND DRAG

The aircraft powerplant provides the force called *thrust* which propels the vehicle

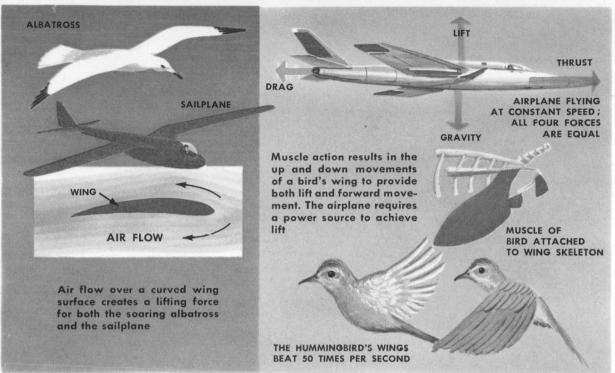

ALBATROSS

SAILPLANE

WING

AIR FLOW

Air flow over a curved wing surface creates a lifting force for both the soaring albatross and the sailplane

Muscle action results in the up and down movements of a bird's wing to provide both lift and forward movement. The airplane requires a power source to achieve lift

LIFT

THRUST

DRAG

GRAVITY

AIRPLANE FLYING AT CONSTANT SPEED; ALL FOUR FORCES ARE EQUAL

MUSCLE OF BIRD ATTACHED TO WING SKELETON

THE HUMMINGBIRD'S WINGS BEAT 50 TIMES PER SECOND

through the air. This thrust must be great enough to start the aircraft in motion and to build up sufficient speed to create lift for flight. Acting against thrust is another force called *drag*. This force is created by the resistance of the air to the forward movement of the aircraft.

All exposed parts of the aircraft create drag. Designers attempt to streamline the entire aircraft to give it a shape which will offer the least resistance to the air. Even small bumps and irregularities in the surface of the aircraft cause a form of drag called *skin friction*. If thrust exceeds drag, the aircraft accelerates. If it is less than the drag, the aircraft slows down.

*An aircraft in level flight at a constant speed and altitude requires that lift must equal gravity and thrust must equal drag.*

### CONTROLS

Aircraft are designed with controls to regulate *lift, pitch* (raising or lowering nose), *roll* (angular motion of wings), and *yaw* (side-to-side motion of nose). The pilot's *throttle* regulates the amount of thrust produced by the engine. This affects the speed of the aircraft and its corresponding lift. *Elevators,* located on the horizontal stabilizer, raise or lower the position of the nose of the aircraft around the axis of pitch. Forward pressure on the control wheel (or *stick*) lowers the nose; a backward movement raises it. The airspeed and attitude of climbing and descending flight are governed by coordinating the throttle and elevator controls. In a gliding descent, for example, thrust is reduced but the desired airspeed is maintained by lowering the nose.

The *ailerons* control the movement of the aircraft around the axis of roll. Pressure to the left on the control stick results in lowering the left wing and raising the right.

The pilot exerts right or left foot pressure on the rudder pedals to control the aircraft movement about the *axis of yaw*. This rudder action is similar to that of a ship and swings the nose of the aircraft right or left.

Control pressures are seldom used separately. The simplest maneuver needs coordination of all three pressures. A simple turn to the right requires coordinated pressures on ailerons, rudder, and elevator.

Aircraft are designed to be properly balanced for flight—to have *inherent stability*—so that the aircraft will tend to fly straight and level with a minimum of control by the pilot. Variations in weight location, speeds, climbing, gliding, and many other factors require the pilot to exert corrective pressures on the controls. To relieve the pilot of this constant control pressure, aircraft are provided with *trim tabs,* small, hinged control surfaces on the main control surfaces. They can be adjusted from the cockpit to balance the forces on the controls.　　R. J. J.

SEE ALSO: AIRCRAFT, AIRPLANE, INSTRUMENT LANDING SYSTEM, INSTRUMENT PANEL

**Flightless birds** see Birds, flightless

**Flint** see Rocks

**A dairy farm flooded by the Columbia River**

**Floe** see Iceberg

**Flood** A flood is the overflowing of water onto land that is normally dry. Most floods occur in spring when heavy rains and melting snow bring more water to streams and rivers than their channels can carry. The extra water flows over surrounding land.

The flooded part of the river valley is called a *flood plain*. Because young rivers have narrow flood plains, their floods do not cover much territory. Mature and older rivers, such as the Nile or the Mississippi, have gradually developed broad flood plains, so their floods cover larger areas.

A single heavy downpour in the narrow valley of a young mountain stream may turn it into a violent torrent within a few hours. This is called a *flash flood*. Great rivers, as the lower course of the Missouri, Ohio and the Mississippi, never have flash floods. Their floods are usually the result of many days of rainfall over large areas.

Floods damage cities and towns, homes and farmlands, and can drown animals and people. Man has found many reasons to move into the flood territory of rivers. Man finds the banks of riverways especially valuable for transportation of goods, for electric power and for rich farmland. In order to use the river banks safely, he has to find ways to control periodic and frequently predictable flooding.

There are several methods of flood prevention. One of these is to build *levees* of sandbags, concrete or other materials. The levees keep the river from overflowing the banks.

Another way is to reduce the amount of water flowing in a river. This is done by building a system of *dams* on the river and its tributaries. The danger of a flood can also be reduced by restoring the natural vegetation that men have destroyed. Grasslands and forests near streams hold water back and are vital to flood control.      C. L. K.
SEE ALSO: DAM, RIVER

**Flora** Flora is the plant population of a particular place or of a certain period of time. The term usually covers all plants of a given region, or during a geological period.
SEE: GEOGRAPHY, GEOLOGIC TIME TABLE, PALEONTOLOGY, PLANT

**Flotation** In the flotation process, crude ORE is ground to a fine powder and placed in a water-oil solution which is stirred to a froth. The lighter materials float off on the froth; other materials settle out.

**Flounder** The flounder is an important food fish for man. Like all of the *flatfish* family, the flounder has an unusual trait. As a baby it looks and swims like all fish. But as it grows, the eyes migrate to one side of the head, right or left, depending on the species. Then it always swims with that side down. The mouth assumes an odd, twisted shape. The skull, or cranium, also turns.

The flounder provides an excellent example of PROTECTIVE COLORATION, as its flat, oval body with spotty appearance is similar to the sand and pebble coloration of the ocean floor.      J. A. D.
SEE ALSO: PISCES

**Starry flounder**

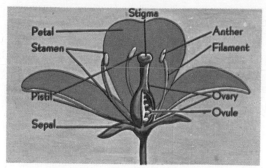

Courtesy Society For Visual Education, Inc.

**Longitudinal-section of a typical flower**

**Petals, stamens and pistil are clearly seen in a dogtooth violet**

Courtesy Society For
Visual Education, Inc.

**Flour** Flour is a food made by grinding WHEAT and other grains. It is classified according to the degree to which it is refined (the bran and other things removed). It is used to make bread, crackers and pastries.

SEE: CEREAL GRAINS

**Flower** A flower is usually a brightly colored part of a plant that produces seeds. Flowers have gay colors and nectar and may be sweet smelling, so that insects and birds are attracted to them and carry their pollen from one plant to another. Flowers are very seldom green, but come in all other colors and combinations of colors. If the flower were green, birds and insects could not tell the flower from the other parts of the plant. The pollen of some plants is carried by the wind.

In a flower there are four main parts. They are the *calyx, corolla, stamen,* and *pistil.* Many flowers do not have all these parts, but a single flower must have either STAMENS or PISTILS, or both, for reproduction. At the base of a flower is a green cup, which is the CALYX. It is composed of leaf-like divisions called *sepals.* The sepals protect the bud and separate when the flower blooms. Within the calyx is the *corolla* or ring of petals. The stamens are inside the corolla. Each stamen is made up of a stalk or *filament* with the pollen-containing *anther* on top. The centermost part is the pistil, with the egg-producing ovary. The *stigma* is at the top of the *style.* When the flower is at the right stage for fertilization, the stigma secretes a sticky substance. It holds any pollen grains that come in contact with it. When pollen is placed on the sticky stigma, it forms a tube-like projection called the pollen tube which grows down into the base of the ovary. When the pollen tube reaches the ovule, a pollen nucleus fertilizes the egg and a seed develops.

Most trees bear flowers, but some are not easily recognized, like the flowers of the cottonwood tree. Many FRUIT trees, such as apple, cherry and orange, have blossoms that are known everywhere for their beauty and fragrance. The flowers of the grasses are the most simple type. ORCHIDS are among the most complicated and beautiful of all flowers. Some flowers, like the rose and buttercup, attract all kinds of insects and birds, but others are constructed so that only certain birds and insects can reach their pollen or nectar.

**Most trees bear flowers**
Courtesy Society For Visual Education, Inc.

All photos courtesy Society For Visual Education, Inc.

Flowers, or blossoms, come in as many varieties as there are flowering plants; for example (top row from left)—blue-eyed grass, a mountain meadow grass; butter-and-eggs, a plant requiring little water; Joshua, a desert tree; (bottom row from left) dandelions, a common wild flower; and trumpet creeper, a climbing vine

All cultivated flowers have been developed from WILD FLOWERS. Wild flowers, usually PERENNIAL, generally grow in woodlands and bloom in early spring. Even the desert has its beautiful wild flowers. When a plant multiplies so rapidly that it becomes a nuisance, it is called a WEED. The hardy, yellow dandelion is such a weed.

Flowers have always been loved and admired by man. Their cultivation, their arrangement, and the development of new varieties, have been interesting to many people. The ancient language of flowers still lives through the giving of flowers as symbols of affection or sympathy. Many nations and states have selected certain flowers as their emblem or symbol. Flowers are often the subject of literature and music.   M. R. L.
SEE ALSO: ANGIOSPERMS, POLLINATION, SEED

**Fluid** A fluid is a substance which is capable of flowing. All liquids and gases are fluids. Air is both a GAS and a fluid; water is both a LIQUID and a fluid.
SEE: SUBSTANCES, PROPERTIES OF

**Fluke** see Liver fluke, Platyhelminthes

**Fluorescent light** see Bulb, electric

**Fluorine** Fluorine is a pale greenish-yellow poisonous GAS. It has a strong odor and eats away almost any moist material. Fluorine will combine with all elements except OXYGEN, the HALOGENS, and inert gases. It is one of the most chemically active elements. Its atomic number is 9, its atomic weight, 19.00. The symbol for fluorine is F.

The chief ores of fluorine are FLUORITE and CRYOLITE. Fluoride compounds are also found in sea water, and bones, nails, and teeth of animals. It is the seventeenth most common element in the earth's crust.

Although fluorine is not rare, it required seventy-five years of experimenting by many scientists before fluorine was finally isolated in 1886 by H. Moissan. He obtained it by passing electricity through liquid hydrogen fluoride with potassium fluoride dissolved in it. The entire experiment had to be done in platinum containers. This same procedure, slightly modified, is used today to obtain free fluorine. While uncombined fluorine is not often used, fluoride compounds have many uses.

Fluorides are added to drinking water in over 1,500 cities throughout the United States. This process is called *fluoridation,* and reduces tooth decay. Only one part of fluoride ion is added to one million parts of water. Too large amounts sometimes cause spotting or mottling of teeth, and concentrated doses of these compounds would be poisonous.

Hydrofluoric acid is used to etch glass, to dissolve the sandy material which plugs boring holes in gas and petroleum wells, to kill wild yeasts in fermentation industries, and to clot rubber latex. In the laboratory, hydrofluoric acid is often used to analyze silicon materials.

Still other compounds of fluorine are used as insecticides and catalysts in chemical reactions.       J. K. L.

SEE ALSO: ELEMENTS

**Fluorite** (FLOO-uh-rite) Fluorite, sometimes called *fluorspar,* is a MINERAL containing CALCIUM and FLUORINE. Fluorite is transparent or translucent stone, and is medium soft and brittle. Varities are white, blue, green, violet or red. Some pieces of fluorite change color as the light strikes them from different angles. They are called *fluorescent.*

The United States is the largest producer of fluorite. It is mined in Illinois, Kentucky, Colorado and New Mexico. Canada and Spain also have large deposits.

Fluorite is used in steel-making to make a fluid slag. It is also used in making enamel for cooking utensils, and in making freon, a refrigerator coolant.       J. K. L.

**Fluorite sample**

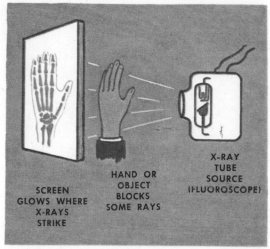

A fluoroscope can reveal the inner structures of organisms and objects

**Fluoroscope** (FLUR-uh-skope) When a person is ill, the physician must first find out the cause of the illness before treatment can be started. Many instruments are used in gathering the necessary information for a proper diagnosis. The fluoroscope is one such instrument. It is especially useful because it allows the physician to observe instantly the shapes of the bones and internal organs of the living body. Fluoroscopy is a painless procedure and can be done in minutes.

The fluoroscope consists of two parts—an X-ray tube and a screen. The usual type of screen is made of cardboard covered with certain fluorescent substances such as barium plastino-cyanide, calcium tungstate or other CRYSTALS. The fluorescent substances change the invisible X-ray radiation into visible light. The screen is covered with lead glass.

The fluoroscope must be used in a darkened room. The patient stands in front of the X-ray tube. The fluorescent screen is placed over the part of the body to be examined. Invisible X-rays are passed through the patient's body. These rays are partially blocked by the bones and internal organs. As a result a shadow image of the organs under examination is cast on the screen. The thicker, more opaque organs cast darker shadows because fewer X-rays are able to pass through them to show up on the fluorescent screen.

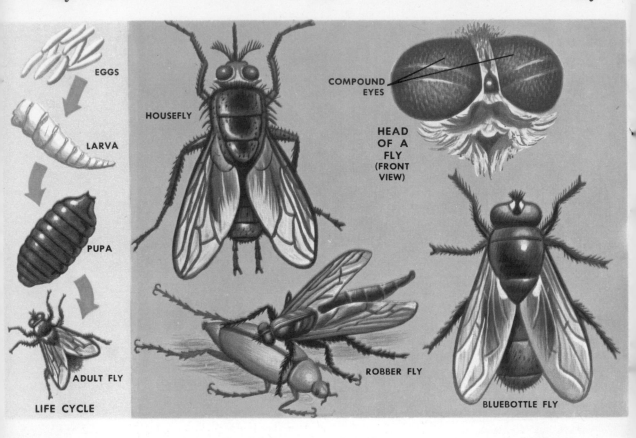

EGGS

LARVA

PUPA

ADULT FLY

LIFE CYCLE

HOUSEFLY

COMPOUND EYES

HEAD OF A FLY (FRONT VIEW)

ROBBER FLY

BLUEBOTTLE FLY

The fluoroscope has been especially useful in the detection of diseases of the LUNGS, the stomach and the heart. Besides its use in diagnosis, it is also useful as an aid to other medical procedures. By using the fluoroscope physicians are able to perform very tedious and difficult tasks, such as medicating the bronchi and removing small tumors without major surgery. This could not be done nearly so easily if the organs remained unseen.

Once the fluoroscope is turned off the picture disappears. This was once considered a distinct disadvantage in the use of the fluoroscope. Today, means of televising the images have been perfected. This provides not only instant observation of internal organs and their responses but also a permanent record of the observation.          G. A. D.

SEE ALSO: MEDICINE, PATHOLOGY, X-RAY

**Fly** Flies are two-winged insects that breed in moist places. Butterflies, dragonflies, and damsel flies are not true flies because they have four wings, as do most other insects.

The *housefly* is the fly that people know best. It breeds in garbage and manure. It then carries the germs of typhoid, DYSENTERY, and cholera on its feet to the food and dishes of man. Proper disposal of refuse and filth and the use of certain chemicals cut down the number of houseflies.

Some flies are helpful to man in pollinating plants and eating other insects, but most flies are dangerous pests. The blood-sucking *tsetse fly* of Africa may carry the fatal SLEEPING SICKNESS. Tiny eye gnats and midges are flies that not only torment, but carry disease.

Warble flies and black flies are harmful to animals. The Mediterranean FRUIT FLY and the Hessian fly harm plants.

Over 85,000 species of flies have been classified and many more remain as yet unidentified. Varieties are found in all countries. The wingless crane fly has been seen on the surface of snow.

A fly has a shell-like exoskeleton. Modi-

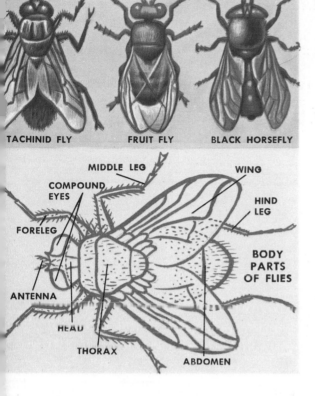

TACHINID FLY    FRUIT FLY    BLACK HORSEFLY

MIDDLE LEG    WING

COMPOUND
EYES    HIND
LEG

FORELEG

BODY
PARTS
OF FLIES

ANTENNA

HEAD

THORAX

ABDOMEN

Reproduction varies with the species. Houseflies lay over a hundred eggs at one time. Some species may lay only one egg and the tsetse fly lays none, but retains her eggs until the pupa stage. The fruit fly produces so many generations so rapidly that it is used in studies of heredity and evolution.

The eggs of the fly turn into slug-like *maggots,* or larvae. The maggots become pupae which soon hatch into full-grown adult flies. Small flies often mistaken for baby houseflies are really adult *tachinid* flies which, unlike the housefly, are beneficial to man by being parasitic upon other insects.

The fly is of the order *Diptera,* from the Greek meaning "two wings."    J. M. C.
SEE ALSO: ARTHROPODA, INSECTA, LARVA, METAMORPHOSIS

**Flycatcher** There are flycatchers all over the world. They are divided into two large groups or families, depending on where they live. All flycatchers are excellent flyers and feed on insects which they catch in flight. Their bills are flat and fringed with bristles which help trap the insects.

One family of flycatchers, the *Muscicapidae,* are found in Europe, Asia, Africa and the South Pacific islands. The members of this family usually build cup-shaped nests either in holes in trees or on tree or bush branches. Some of the Asian species are very brightly colored and adorned with crests, plumes or fantails. Many of them have loud sweet songs.

The American flycatchers, *tyrant* fly-catchers, are found in warm climates. The large species, the *kingbirds* and *great crested flycatcher,* are grayish birds with yellow or white breasts. The smaller species, including the PEEWEE, are similar in color and generally call their names rather than sing.    E. R. B.

fications of the two missing wings are called *halteres* and are rod-shaped organs used for balance in flight. Flies have compound eyes and sometimes three auxiliary eyes called *ocelli*. They eat by means of a *proboscis*— a long sucking tube that includes the mouth. The fly breathes through holes along its body called *spiracles*.

Flies can walk upside down on the ceiling because their feet have cushions, called *pulvilli,* which attach themselves to smooth surfaces by tiny sticky hairs.

**Crane fly**

Buchsbaum

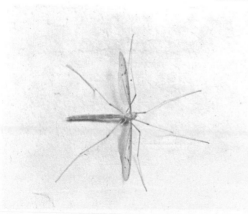

**An American flycatcher**

**ALFRED B. NOBEL**
1833–1896 •
Invented dynamite,
started Nobel Prizes

**HIPPOCRATES**
460–370? B.C •
"Father of Medicine"

**MARIE CURIE**
• 1867–1934
Discovered radium
and polonium

**ENRICO FERMI**
• 1901–1954
Produced first atomic pile and first
controlled nuclear chain reaction

**THOMAS ALVA EDISON**
1847–1931 •
Invented light bulb,
phonograph and mimeograph

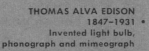

**NICOLAUS COPERNICUS**
• 1473–1543
First astronomer to say that Earth
goes around the sun

**LUTHER BURBANK**
• 1849–1926
Invented new
varieties of plants

**EDWARD JENNER**
1749–1823 •
Discovered smallpox vaccine

**CHARLES DARWIN**
1809-1882 •
Conceived the Theory of Evolution
through Natural Selection

**WILLIAM HARVEY**
• 1578–1657
Discovered the circulation
of the blood

**GEORGE WASHINGTON CARVER**
1864–1943 •
Experimented with
practical botany

**SAMUEL F. B. MORSE**
• 1791–1872
Invented telegraph and Morse code

**LOUIS PASTEUR**
• 1822–1895
Invented pasteurization

**BENJAMIN FRANKLIN**
• 1706–1790
Invented lightning rod